Free from the Past

McDougal & Associates
Servants of Christ and stewards of the mysteries of God

Free from the Past

Laugh and Cry Your Way to FREEDOM

by

John Chappell

FREE FROM THE PAST
Copyright © 2009 by John R. Chappell, III
ALL RIGHTS RESERVED

No part of this book may be reproduced or transmitted in any form or by any means, electronic or mechanical, including photocopying, recording, or by any information retrieval system.

All Scripture references are from the Authorized King James Version of the Bible, unless otherwise noted. References marked NKJ are from the New King James Version of the Bible, copyright © 1979, 1980, 1982, by Thomas Nelson, Inc., Nashville, Tennessee.

The testimonies we have used as examples are based on actual events. Names of persons and places have been changed to ensure the privacy of the individuals involved.

This book was originally published in 2000 under the title *Laugh and Cry Your Way to Freedom*. This McDougal & Associates edition has been revised, updated and expanded, has been totally re-typeset and has a new cover design.

Published by:

McDougal & Associates
www.thepublishedword.com

McDougal & Associates is dedicated to the spreading of the Gospel of Jesus Christ to as many people as possible in the shortest time possible.

ISBN 13: 978-1-934769-17-1
ISBN 10: 1-934769-17-7

Printed in the United States of America
For Worldwide Distribution

Acknowledgments

Free from the Past, a book on inner healing, deliverance and the renewed mind, would not have been possible without the rich heritage we received under the ministry of Wallace H. Heflin, Sr., his wife, Edith Ward Heflin, and their amazing daughter, Ruth Heflin, missionary to the world. I also learned much from Ruth's brother, Wallace H. Heflin, Jr., particularly during our overseas trips together.

This book came forth out of nearly thirty-eight years of ministry to the inner healing needs of others in partnership with my lovely wife Pattie. Many creative ideas and important editorial changes have come from our daughter, Margaret. In the early years of the book's development, Bonnie Bailey graciously typed several inner healing tapes for me, and I am grateful for this help.

Pattie and I learned invaluable information on inner healing, particularly in connection with soul ties and fragmentation, from our Australian friend Leone Watson and her late husband Ron. We are grateful to them also for setting up our itinerary in that country during 1991-1993.

I gained much knowledge in the area of inner healing from several Christian authors, particularly from books by John and Paula Sandford.

Finally, my thanks to the many brothers and sisters in Christ who have supported the ministry and greatly encouraged and prayed for us through the years.

Contents

Preface 9
Introduction 11

1. Inner Healing: What Is It and Who Needs It? 17
2. The Baptism in the Holy Spirit and Inner Healing ... 35
3. Inner Healing through Self-Travail 53
4. Inner Healing through Holy Laughter 61
5. Inner Healing through Forgiveness 81
6. Breaking the Power of Generational Iniquity 93
7. Breaking the Power of Destructive Inner Vows ... 113
8. Negative Soul Ties, Idolatry and Fragmentation .. 123
9. The Renewed Mind and Inner Healing 141
10. Easy Steps to Life-Transforming Inner Healing
    (and Deliverance) 161

Appendix:
   How to Receive the Baptism in the Holy Spirit
   and the Gift of Speaking in Other Tongues 173

Ministry Page 181

Preface

Free from the Past has a twofold purpose. The first and primary purpose is that you may become more fully healed and set free from the hurts, rejection and other strongholds in your life, which prevent you from becoming the person God created you to be. The second purpose is to enable you to minister inner healing and deliverance to others, that they may become whole persons and fulfill their God-given destinies.

With these goals in mind, the book is designed to transform the lives of those who read it. Each chapter is broken down into small sections. If, while you are reading, you recall a painful memory, perhaps something you haven't thought about for years, stop reading and take the remembered hurt before the Lord. Give Him the rejection, the hurt, the broken relationship and the abuse. Let the tears and even the deep crying come. Pray and forgive others, yourself and even God until joy comes. Also take a look at Chapter 10. This chapter will help you to be set free. Then, when you feel release and have gotten the victory, continue reading to learn and experience more. As you read through the book, do this again and again as necessary so that you can truly be *Free from the Past*.

Introduction

Since 1973, my wife, Pattie, and I have been deeply involved in the inner healing ministry, a ministry of the Holy Spirit that produces a deep inner change within us Christian believers so that we are progressively cleansed, healed within and conformed to the image of Christ. The theological term for this change is sanctification. This ministry sets us free from various emotional and relationship problems that may have been caused by abuse, rejection or other crippling events of the past.

The result is that we are enabled to receive deeply the forgiveness of God, and then we can forgive ourselves. We are freed from unforgiveness toward others, toward God and toward ourselves. This, in turn, frees us from bitterness and wrong attitudes so that we can become the loving individuals God has created us to be. Holy laughter and deep travailing crying are keys to life-changing releases from past hurts and rejection. I refer to this type of travail as "self-travail," to differentiate it from the act of travailing for others.

Over the past thirty-five years, we have seen the Lord Jesus, through the mighty power of the Holy Spirit, liberate thousands of Christians to walk in new intimacy with God. Life-transforming changes in their lives and joyful, fulfilling relationships with others have been the result.

It has been through these years of experience that this book is birthed. The desire of my heart is to see you, the reader, and many others like you liberated in a similar fashion. I believe that you are not reading this book by chance. Some of you have exhausted every means for help. You have experienced one disaster after another in your life, and you are about to give up. God has the answer for you in this book. We have seen one "impossible" case after another set free by the Holy Spirit. This is a divine appointment, an answer to the cry of your heart to be changed, to be set free, so that you can walk *"in newness of life."*

Some of you may be reading this book because you have a desire to be more effective in setting others free from such spiritual hindrances. In either case, I believe your desire will be fulfilled.

A few years after becoming involved in the inner healing ministry, I found, to my surprise, that almost all Christians were oppressed to some extent by evil spirits, and some to a great extent. We thank God for using us to help Christians be delivered from such oppressions.

I am not suggesting that these people were demon possessed. As born-again Christians, we cannot be demon-possessed, nor have an evil spirit abiding within our own spirits. We can, however, be oppressed by evil spirits in our souls (the realm of our natural emotions, mind and will) and, as a result, need to be set free. In most cases, such oppression results from having some form of sin in our lives or from having been sinned against. Repentance and forgiveness of others, or both, are usually essential keys to deliverance.

This ministry has changed my own life. I have been astonished at the dimension of pride, rebellion, deception, jealousy, unforgiveness, rage, unbelief and other areas of darkness the Spirit has helped me to see in myself and overcome through the years. Through inner healing God has made one change after another in my life, and through His grace, I now have deep peace and joy within and walk in a new dimension of intimacy with the Lord Jesus.

The Christian life is meant to be beautiful and exciting, and although we are all far from perfect, the Lord is ready to make many much-needed changes in us. When we are changed, then we have a responsibility through the Holy Spirit to help change others.

In the pages of this book, I want to share with you some of the simple, yet life-changing, truths that have turned my life and the lives of thousands of others around. I know that, as you cooperate with the Holy Spirit and hunger to be changed, the knowledge in this book will revolutionize your life as well. God loves you and has a plan for you to be *Free from the Past*.

In our own ministry, we have found that we can minister inner healing and deliverance in several different ways. Sometimes it is by mass prayer for a large group of people, and many lives have been changed in this way. Whenever possible, however, we give special attention to each individual, and this is usually even more effective.

However, you can be set free from the hurts, rejections and heartache of the past without anyone else praying for you. You will discover that, through some simple, Holy Spirit-inspired methods or principles, you can be released from rage, lust, depression and fear and from being a victim or a victimizer of others. You can have victory in all of these areas because the Word of God states clearly: *"In all these things we are more than conquerors through him that loved us"* (Romans 8:37).

It is my hope that this book will be used to raise up and equip teachers, who will have inner healing/deliverance ministries and who, in turn, will teach others to have similar ministries. In this way, the entire Body of Christian believers throughout the world will be benefited.

When I use the expression "inner healing" in this book, my intention will always be to include deliverance from evil spirits. The two ministries are different, but they are intertwined; they work together. Inner healing is usually needed for deliverance to be lasting. Although much deliverance will occur automatically when one experiences inner healing, there are many occasions when specific, powerful prayer is needed for complete deliverance.

The principles and methods you read about in this book are scriptural and Holy Spirit-inspired, and they have set thousands free. We have used all of them over a period of many years, so we know they work. Now you can use them to be set free yourself and to help free others. Let them be tools for the glory of God and for the upbuilding of His Kingdom.

Now, turn to Chapter 1 and see what exciting things the Lord has in store for you.

John Chappell
Bartow, Florida

Chapter 1

Inner Healing:
What is it and Who Needs It?

Surely he hath borne our griefs, and carried our sorrows. ... He was wounded for our transgressions, he was bruised for our iniquities: the chastisement of our peace was upon him; and with his stripes we are healed. Isaiah 53:4-5

FREE FROM THE PAST

> *Fred had suffered, as so many have, the childhood abuse of not having been held in his parents' arms and of not having been verbally told he was loved!*

The Spirit of the Lord is upon me, because he hath anointed me to preach the gospel to the poor; he hath sent me to heal the brokenhearted, to preach deliverance to the captives, and recovering of sight to the blind, to set at liberty them that are bruised. Luke 4:18

He healeth the broken in heart, and bindeth up their wounds.
Psalm 147:3

ANNE: SEXUALLY ABUSED BY HER BROTHERS

"I was sexually abused by my two brothers when I was a child and raped as a teenager," Anne told us. "Then I went through two physically abusive marriages." Pattie and I ministered inner healing to Anne, as she sobbed deeply. We broke the soul ties with her abusers and prayed deliverance over her from various spirits.

"Through the Chappells' ministry to me," she later testified, "I was able to deeply forgive my two brothers and my two ex-husbands.

Inner Healing: What Is It and Who Needs It?

I felt so free, so different, so peaceful." There was indeed a marvelous change in Anne's life. All bitterness, shame and self-pity left her, and she glowed all over, filled with the peace and love of God. This is what the Lord does for His children through inner healing, and He will do it for you too.

Fred: Unloved by His Parents

Fred was raised on a dairy farm. He had good, moral, hard-working parents, who provided him with a stable home, delicious farm-cooked meals, fine clothing and a good education. Fred said, "I thought I had a near-perfect childhood and didn't understand why my emotions were so imprisoned, so suppressed." This is typical of many of us. Fred had suffered, as so many have, the childhood abuse of not having been held in his parents' arms and of not having been verbally told he was loved.

As we ministered inner healing to Fred, one by one his emotional walls began to crumble, and his suppressed emotions, including rage, began to be released. "Wow! What a change I feel!" he told us. "I feel so released inside!" You may need that same release.

Helen: Traumatized by Her Husband's Infidelity

"Eight years ago my husband broke my heart through an affair with another woman. He has deeply repented, and I know he loves me, and I love him. I have tried to forgive him and forget what happened," said Helen, "but my pain is so deep that when we come together in the marriage bed, I cannot give myself physically to him."

"Will you pray for me?" she pleaded. "I want to be set free from the thoughts of what my husband did so that I can have a normal marriage."

I got ready to lay my hands on Helen's head, but the Holy Spirit stopped me. "Don't pray for the relationship with her husband now," the Lord showed me. "Pray for Helen's relationship with her father, for that is the root of the problem."

I prayed for Helen to be healed of the deep hurts she had suffered through her father's rejection. For thirty minutes she cried deeply through the pains of his rejection. Then she felt a forgiveness and love for her father birthed within her. She told us, "Having been set free of unforgiveness toward my father, I was amazed that all unforgiveness toward my husband was also gone. From that day, I was free to love and trust my husband and even to trust God more deeply." I can remember so clearly that when Helen and her husband left the meeting that day, they looked like honeymooners.

If, like Anne, Fred and Helen, you have been damaged by life, you also can be set *Free from the Past*. Start now!

WE HUMANS ARE TRIUNE BEINGS

We humans are triune beings. We are a spirit, we possess a soul (the realm of the emotions, mind and will), and we live in a body. It is our spirits that are reborn at salvation. When we invite Jesus to come into our hearts, we are born again, made *"new creatures"* in Christ. Our spirit, which was dead in sin, becomes alive in God. We are now one spirit with the Lord (see 1 Corinthians 6:17).

It is within the soul realm that we find things that are still displeasing to God: pride, rebellion, fear, lust, unbelief, unforgiveness, rage, jealousy, emotional pain, rejection and many other areas of darkness. A vast amount of inner healing and deliverance from evil spirits is needed to achieve the abundant, victorious life God has promised to each of us.

Some call the ministry of inner healing "soul healing" because it is healing that takes place in the soul of a person, primarily in the emotions. Jesus came to set men free, and He does it through inner healing.

Some call the inner healing ministry simply "restoration" because it involves a restoring, or making new, of the soul. As David said, *"He restoreth my soul"* (Psalm 23:3). God is still in the restoration business.

Others call this ministry "the healing of memories" because the emotional pains and poisons from old memories are removed through inner healing.

Still others call this ministry "death and rebirth" because it is, in fact, an appropriation of Christ's death and resurrection for us. As Saint Paul declared in Galatians 2:20, *"I am crucified with Christ: nevertheless I live."* Death to our old nature, including sinful strongholds within us, frees us from destructive influences. We are freed to follow the will of God and to fulfill our divine destinies.

By any name, this ministry involves a healing of the inner man, distinguishing it from outward or physical healing, the healing of the body. It is the healing of emotional, mental and physical abuse, usually inflicted in the early years of our lives by parents or other family members or friends.

Hurts, trauma and rejection, especially the ones suffered in our childhood years, damage us emotionally and can prevent us from becoming the people God has created us to be. The bad fruit that develops from these childhood hurts includes unforgiveness, bitterness, insecurity, wrong attitudes, sexual sins and various emotional problems. In the atonement, Jesus has taken these deep hurts, sorrows and griefs of the past and has purchased both physical and inner healing for us through His shed blood. The purpose of the inner healing ministry is to set us free from the results of such abuse and rejection and to enable us to enjoy fulfilling, victorious lives. Through inner healing, we are liberated from being victims of the past and are able to become *"more than conquerors"* in Christ (Romans 8:37).

From God's dealings in my own life, and from our experience in ministering to thousands of Christians for more than three decades, Pattie and I have learned many new things about the inner healing ministry. What we have found in the Body of Christ in general has surprised us.

ALL OF US NEED INNER HEALING

All of us need a great deal of inner healing. Wounded

Inner Healing: What Is It and Who Needs It?

and hurting Christians need far more inner healing than I originally believed necessary. Many Christians have a reservoir of unhealed hurts and hidden rage. This may even include those who have already received much inner healing. Therefore all of us need to know how to receive inner healing and deliverance on a continuing basis. This is a lifetime undertaking, part of the continual work of inner sanctification, the process of being conformed to the image of Christ.

Pastors, deacons and even well-known Christian leaders fall into sexual and financial sins (and it happens everywhere in the world and in every denomination). Many of them desperately desire help, but they don't know where to go to get that help.

Living in Denial

Others, who know about the inner healing ministry but refuse to seek it for themselves, are simply denying that they need help. The truth is that few of us want to face our need for repentance, inner healing and perhaps even deliverance. We prefer to hide from God and from ourselves. The very thought of being needy can be frightening to us. We like

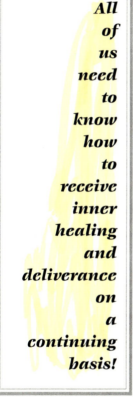

All of us need to know how to receive inner healing and deliverance on a continuing basis!

to feel that we pretty much "have it together" and are in control of our lives. The denied problems of rejection, insecurity, rage, lust, depression, self-hatred, dishonesty and addictions therefore go underground, only to surface later in destructive ways. These include broken marriages, deeply wounded children and destroyed ministries. Jesus is ready to set us free from all emotional hang-ups and paralyzing memories of the past.

We blame others, circumstances, our parents and even God, but refuse to accept any responsibility ourselves. I am speaking from experience, for I have been guilty of much of the above. We are all guilty of this, and usually to a great degree. It is our nature to deny our need. The Bible declares:

> *The heart is deceitful above all things, and desperately wicked: who can know it?*   Jeremiah 17:9

None of us can know our own heart without a revelation from the Holy Spirit. The Lord is willing and eager to show us our hearts, but we must cooperate with Him. If we're willing, He will reveal to us the dark areas, the sins, the negative mind-sets, the traditions of man and the weaknesses that need to be cleansed, changed and removed. He tells us:

> *I the LORD search the heart, I try the reins, even to give every man according to his ways, and according to the fruit of his doings.*   Jeremiah 17:10

Inner Healing: What Is It and Who Needs It?

It is time to drop all pretense and to face the painful truth. I can teach on denial because I experienced it. It took me many years to be able to admit the painful truth that my father never told me he loved me and seldom hugged me. Since then, I have spent hours in prayer being freed from this painful rejection. With the inner healing I experienced as a result, I have moved into a whole new place of peace and joy, and I have developed a more intimate relationship with God and with others.

My Extensive Anger List

Some years ago, while I was teaching about the enormous amount of unforgiveness and buried anger every person has, God gave me a surprising revelation. Like most Christians, I thought I had already forgiven everyone. I was sure that hidden anger was no problem in my own life. The Spirit of God, however, had a different idea about how anger-free I was. He showed me twenty-one different people against whom I still harbored unforgiveness and resentment. Some of this resentment went back twenty and even forty years. I had mentally forgiven most of the people on that list, but God requires heart forgiveness.

When the Lord revealed this to me, I had a long prayer session, and one by one God set me free from my unforgiveness toward each of the twenty-one people. This experience brought a wonderful new peace into my life. We all need inner healing. We all need to forgive more deeply.

The Prevalent Spirit of Lust

> *From seventy-five to ninety-five percent of all Christian men and perhaps as many as fifty percent of all Christian women need deliverance from the evil spirit of lust!*

To my astonishment, I have found that anywhere from seventy-five to ninety-five percent of all Christian men and perhaps as many as fifty percent of all Christian women need deliverance from the evil spirit of lust. I have been delivered from it myself, and I am now free. How about you? Such spirits attack the thought-life of the believer and often lead them into pornography and other forms of immorality.

Once, when I was teaching a Sunday school class of thirty born-again Christian men, twenty-seven of them confessed to having a substantial problem with lustful thoughts, and three or four of them confessed that those lustful thoughts plagued them throughout the day every day. Only one or two of those men knew how to get victory.

In a marriage seminar that we held, eight of the ten men present expressed their need for deliverance from a spirit of lust.

In both of these groups, the men repented and asked God to deliver them. I prayed for them, and they were set free from lust. They reported feeling a great change within, and it became much easier for them to avoid lustful thoughts after that.

In an overseas meeting that Pattie and I conducted, fifteen pastors and leaders expressed a desire for deliverance from a spirit of lust. These pastors repented, and through the power of the Holy Spirit, God delivered each one of them.

Those who want to remain free from such bondages must consistently cast down all negative imaginations, speak only holy, faith words, study and meditate on the Word of God, and spend time daily praying in other tongues.

We Must Change

As we noted earlier, we usually blame either other people or outward circumstances—or both—for the difficulties and disappointments in our lives and even for our personal failures. We must be courageous and recognize that *we* are the ones who need to change, not others. We are called to be more than conquerors through Christ Jesus, and it is inward change—being conformed to the image of Christ—that will lead us to a life of victory and joy. If we continue to deny the truth of our need to change, we prevent God from transforming us into His image, and we reject the very thing that will bring healing and fulfillment into our lives.

FREE FROM THE PAST

Even if you have received much inner healing and deliverance from the Lord, you almost certainly need much more. Here are some signs indicating such a need:

1. You were not hugged, cuddled, embraced or told verbally that you were loved by one or both of your parents.
2. As a child, you were abused mentally, emotionally or sexually. This includes abuse through religious legalism. It also includes having to earn love and not receiving it unconditionally.
3. You had a one-parent family, alcoholic parent(s) or the divorce of your parents during your childhood.
4. You have had a painful teenage period or marriage(s.)
5. You have one or more compulsions or addictions to things such as alcohol, drugs, food, gambling, work, sexual fantasies, rage, soap operas or over-spending.
6. You have many negative, critical, jealous or fearful thoughts, or you have a habit of boasting or putting others down verbally.
7. You have many lustful thoughts or habits.
8. You have undergone one or more abortions.
9. You experience rebellion against authority figures.
10. You suffer from constant marital problems.
11. You experience much stress in your life.
12. You easily lose your temper with loved ones (or others). This may be the tip of the iceberg of much underlying pain, fear, rage and insecurity.

13. You experience feelings of inferiority, depression or sadness. Also, there is a lack of peace and joy in your life.
14. You exhibit dishonesty, lying or exaggeration.
15. You were involved in the occult before salvation. This includes ouija boards, palm reading, astrology, séances, rock music, witchcraft and horror TV and movies.

Put a check mark beside each of these fifteen that applies to you. Then read Chapter 10, and take the easy steps to life-transforming inner healing that are outlined there.

Did You Really Have a Good Childhood?

You may insist that you had a perfectly wonderful childhood, but tell me, how often did your father hug you? How often did he sit you on his lap and tell you he loved you? The answer, in my own life and perhaps in yours as well, is "never" or "not very often."

How about your mother? Did she hug you or tell you she loved you often? Your answer may be, "We just weren't that kind of family!" If that is true, then a lack of hearing those heartfelt words "I love you" and experiencing frequent hugs and kisses from your parents has had a powerful negative effect on your life—whether you have realized it or not.

Because your parents provided you food and clothing, and they didn't abuse you physically, you may have thought you had a good childhood. However, if you were not hugged and frequently told you were loved, there is a great emotional wound within you, an emotional vacuum. This causes suppressed emotions, insecurity and inner rage. You need to be healed from this wound and delivered from the rage within. Jesus will fill up that empty place in your heart with His love.

The Trauma of the Teen Years and Its Aftermath

For most people, the teenage period is a time of questioning and experimentation. During this time, many young people investigate the supernatural. Unfortunately, it is usually the occult rather than the supernatural working of the Holy Spirit, as most teens are not aware that godly supernatural gifts even exist. Many teenagers get involved with Eastern religions, use ouija boards, study horoscopes and astrology, have séances or visit palm readers. Such involvement opens them up to evil spirits that can plague them for the rest of their lives, and they need to be deeply ministered to through inner healing and deliverance.

During their teenage years, many make wrong choices, and this brings about trauma and emotional pain from which some never fully recover. When teenagers experiment with sex, they forge a negative bonding to their sex partners, damage their emotions and harden their conscience to sin. Their hearts are fragmented and

INNER HEALING: WHAT IS IT AND WHO NEEDS IT?

torn. Such sexual experiences also negatively influence a person's thought-life.

If this describes you, and you are now married, most likely it has been difficult for you to bond deeply with your marriage partner. The more sexual affairs you had in the past, the harder it is for you to have the close bonding desired with your spouse. It is like a piece of adhesive tape. Each time you use it, it loses some of its ability to stick. When you lose your ability to stick emotionally to your marriage partner, you subconsciously find yourself looking around for someone else to love. The soul ties that develop from premarital sexual partners need to be broken, your damaged, fragmented soul needs to be healed, and you need to be set free from guilt feelings and shame.

> *If you were not hugged and frequently told you were loved, there is a great emotional wound within you!*

The Bible tells us that *"two become one"* in marriage. In the sexual relationship, married or not, you become one with your partner. During sexual union, evil spirits from one partner are transferred to the other, and we need deliverance from these evil spirits.

FREE FROM THE PAST

DAMAGE FROM EXTENDED GRIEF OVER THE DEATH OF LOVED ONES

The death of key people in your life results in deep emotional pain. When a loved one dies, our society discourages us from properly grieving. Tears of grief, which might normally continue for weeks or even months, disturb those around us. Yet such tears (unless carried on for too long) are necessary for our mental and emotional health. The vast majority of us have not cried nearly enough for the death of our loved ones. Therefore, much of the grief and emotional pain remains. This produces many negative side effects in your life, including stress, arthritis, hidden resentment, depression and even negative soul ties with your deceased loved ones.

DAMAGE FROM VERBAL ABUSE IN CHILDHOOD

When we were small children, we believed whatever our parents told us. They were like God to us. Children are wounded deeply when their parents speak negative words like "You're stupid," "You're no good," or "You will never amount to much." Such negative words become established in our hearts and become a curse upon our life. If the curse of such words is not broken, it will hinder you greatly throughout the entire course of your life.

At first, you may be succeeding at your job, in your business, in your marriage or in your ministry, but for some reason you repeatedly do something that causes you to fail. This is a curse, and it needs to be broken

INNER HEALING: WHAT IS IT AND WHO NEEDS IT?

through inner healing and deliverance. As we shall see, you also need to start substituting words of faith for the negative statements that have dominated your life until now. Your mind must be changed, renewed by the Word of God, made to see things the way God sees them.

DAMAGE FROM SEXUAL ABUSE IN CHILDHOOD

Abuse can be mental, emotional or physical. Statistics show that about one out of four girls and a high percentage of boys under the age of ten have been abused sexually in this country. This abuse is usually carried out by one of their own family members, a friend of the family or a neighbor. As these children mature, they critically need inner healing if they are to be free to function as emotionally healthy adults.

Sexual abuse marks one as a victim and, like a powerful magnet, draws further abuse into one's life. A girl who has been sexually abused in the early years will often be abused or even raped as a teenager. There seems to be a sign over such children identifying them as potential targets. This can be explained. Through the process of transference from the abuser, this child has received a seducing spirit and a spirit of lust. He or she is usually unaware of having such a spirit, but this evil spirit draws, or seduces, potential abusers or rapists.

THE CONCLUSION

Any person who has marriage problems, insecurity,

rage, lust, depression, stress, self-hatred, fears, negativity, dishonesty or addictions is in need of inner healing and/or deliverance. Preachers and evangelists who desire to preach with brokenness and compassion are in need of inner healing and/or deliverance. All those who desire to be more intimate with God and more intimate, vulnerable and transparent with their loved ones and with others are in need of inner healing and/or deliverance. I need it; you need it; we all need it.

The chapters that follow will reveal how easily and quickly you can receive inner healing and, through it, become the person God has created you to be. You, too, can be *Free from the Past!*

Why don't you begin now by turning to Chapter 10 and taking the easy steps outlined there to help you obtain inner healing?

Chapter 2

The Baptism in the Holy Spirit and Inner Healing

But ye shall receive power, after that the Holy Ghost is come upon you.   Acts 1:8

And when the day of Pentecost was fully come, ... they were all filled with the Holy Ghost, and began to speak with other tongues, as the Spirit gave them utterance.   Acts 2:1-4

FREE FROM THE PAST

And the same day there were added unto them about three thousand souls.   Acts 2:41

OUR PERSONAL DAY OF PENTECOST

On June 24, 1967, Pattie and I received Jesus into our hearts. That same night we were baptized in the Holy Spirit, and both of us spoke in tongues. Pattie said this: "I spoke in three different languages. I also had several visions, received words of knowledge about friends of ours and felt the arms of Jesus go around me. I even received a healing in my body. All pain in my wrists, shoulders and elbows left. It was a life-changing experience for me."

Aside from the brief lull I will mention later in the book, I have never stopped speaking in tongues since that day. We worship the Lord in tongues daily and intercede in tongues for ourselves and for others. Being baptized in the Holy Spirit has given us a deep love for the Lord Jesus Christ, a love for the Bible and for prayer and a greater love and compassion for others. It has brought great joy and fulfillment into our lives and a ministry that has taken us to more than forty nations of the world.

BILL'S TESTIMONY OF WALKING THROUGH THE SECOND DOOR

Bill approached me one evening at church and said, "Brother Chappell, I've been saved for five years, I love

The Baptism in the Holy Spirit and Inner Healing

the Lord, and I get such a joy out of my ministry of feeding the poor. Every day I read my Bible and pray, but still I feel a hunger for more of God. I want to be baptized in the Holy Spirit now. Will you pray for me?"

"Surely I will," I said to Bill. "Raise your head high, and see Jesus on the cross. Yes, picture Him on the cross." I then instructed Bill to repeatedly praise God loudly with the words, "I love You, Jesus." When he had begun to do this, I then laid my hand on his head.

Later Bill testified to others, "I felt a warm feeling going all through me, and my words of praise in English changed to words I didn't understand. I was speaking in an unknown language. I soon spoke in a second and then a third unknown language. How awesome! With each language, I felt more of the presence of God. I didn't know anyone could feel so close to Him. Soon after that I found I had the power of God in my life also!"

> *All pain in my wrists, shoulders and elbows left!*

A few months after being filled with Holy Spirit, Bill said, "The Bible has come alive to me. I have visions and hear God's voice many times each day. I am experiencing His glorious presence much of the time, and it has changed my entire life."

FREE FROM THE PAST

FIFTY DAYS AFTER OUR LORD'S RESURRECTION — THE DAY OF PENTECOST

Forty days after His resurrection, Jesus ascended to Heaven. On that momentous day, He commanded His disciples:

> *Tarry [wait] ye in the city of Jerusalem, until ye be endued with power from on high.*   Luke 24:49

After Jesus had gone, the disciples returned to Jerusalem and went into an upper room. Ten days later, on the Jewish feast day of Pentecost, about one hundred and twenty of the disciples, including Mary, the mother of Jesus, were baptized in the Holy Spirit in that upper room. The Holy Spirit came into that room like a mighty, powerful wind. At the same time, purifying, sanctifying tongues of fire came upon them all, and they all spoke in other tongues. It was a life-transforming experience of great power and inner change.

In the Bible, the infilling of the Holy Spirit always appears to have been accompanied by two things—by a mighty inner transformation and by speaking in other tongues. On the Day of Pentecost, all those who received spoke in other tongues. Paul spoke in other tongues when he received the baptism of the Spirit in Damascus. When those who had gathered at the house of Cornelius in Caesarea were filled with the Holy Spirit, they also spoke in tongues (see Acts 10:46). When the apostle Paul laid hands on the disciples of John the Baptist at

THE BAPTISM IN THE HOLY SPIRIT AND INNER HEALING

Ephesus, they were baptized in the Holy Spirit, *"and they spake with tongues, and prophesied"* (Acts 19:6).

The baptism in the Holy Spirit with speaking in other tongues is the key to a deeper prayer life and to a more intimate relationship with the Lord Jesus. The Word of God comes alive when it is quickened to you by the Spirit, you are able to hear the voice of God more easily, and visions come to you more freely. We should get our children filled with the Spirit at an early age. One of ours was filled at age five, one at six and one at ten. Because of this, all of them began hearing the voice of God and having visions while they were very young.

The baptism in the Holy Spirit immediately gives you a greater anointing to minister to others, whether it is in preaching, teaching, singing, witnessing, praying for the sick or delivering the oppressed. So the sooner you can receive it, the better.

New converts and millions of Christians in every denomination and in every nation are receiving the baptism in the Holy Spirit and speaking in other tongues. Fifteen years ago it was already estimated that there were 240 million or more Spirit-filled believers worldwide. People are hungry for this experience, as it brings more power, joy and a greater love for Jesus into the lives of all those who receive it.

FROM COWARDICE TO HOLY BOLDNESS

And when she saw Peter warming himself, she looked upon him, and said, And thou also wast with Jesus of Nazareth. But he denied ... .

FREE FROM THE PAST

And he denied it again. ... He began to curse and to swear, saying, I know not this man of whom ye speak.
Mark 14:67-68 and 70-71

The baptism in the Holy Spirit delivers us from fear and makes us bold. Peter denied Jesus three times and even cursed during the third denial. Then, on the Day of Pentecost, this same Peter was baptized in the Holy Spirit and fire, and the Lord delivered him from a spirit of fear and from profanity. That day his fears were replaced by a courage that would enable him, in the future, to preach the Gospel all over the known world in the face of imprisonment and death. Peter's life was totally changed that day.

> *The baptism in the Holy Spirit delivers us from fear and makes us bold!*

When Jesus was arrested, Peter was not the only one who denied Him:

Then all the disciples forsook him, and fled.
Matthew 26:56
(see also Mark 14:50)

On the Day of Pentecost, these other disciples were also baptized in the Holy Spirit and fire and delivered from their fears. Their lives were dramatically changed, and they, too, became willing to suffer and die for the Lord.

Paul's life was cleansed, sanctified and empowered through the baptism of the Holy Spirit and speaking in other tongues. As a result, he declared, *"I thank my God, I speak with tongues more than ye all"* (1 Corinthians 14:18). His whole life had been totally turned around. His former hatred of Christians was now transformed into a burning love for Christ and His people, and his driving energy to persecute and destroy Christians changed into a zeal to win souls for Christ. He was able to declare:

> *I count all things but loss for the excellency of the knowledge of Christ Jesus my Lord: for whom I have suffered the loss of all things, and do count them but dung, that I may win Christ.*   Philippians 3:8

In the time of the early Church, virtually everyone (including the authors of the New Testament books, all the apostles and even Mary the mother of Jesus) had this experience of being baptized in the Holy Spirit and speaking in other tongues. Through the baptism in the Holy Spirit, the Lord did a deep work of inner transformation and sanctification (inner healing) in Peter, in Paul and in the lives of the other disciples.

These all became *"obedient unto death"* and were transformed into firebrands for their faith. Their heart's desire became winning souls for Christ. If you have not yet been baptized in the Holy Spirit, including speaking in other tongues, please proceed to the

Appendix and follow the instructions given there. You need this experience.

Different Dimensions of Being Baptized in the Holy Spirit

There are different dimensions of being baptized in the Holy Spirit, and most of us are receiving experiences far below the level God has for us. We should not be satisfied with a "light" infilling of the Holy Spirit. I speak from experience, for I received a light infilling myself. I wanted a deeper experience, so I went on a ten-day fast, and on the third day of the fast I received a life-changing refilling of the Spirit, which included deliverance from an occultic evil spirit.

According to the Bible pattern, the baptism in the Holy Spirit is accompanied by a dramatic transformation in one's life, with the purifying, transforming fire of the Holy Spirit attending it. John the Baptist declared:

> *I indeed baptize you with water; but one mightier than I cometh, the latchet of whose shoes I am not worthy to unloose: he shall baptize you with the Holy Ghost and with fire.* Luke 3:16

The *"fire"* of the Holy Spirit produces much cleansing and inner healing in those who experience it.

Three Days of Holy Laughter, Three Days of Weeping

One elderly Australian minister told me, "I laughed off

and on for three days after being baptized in the Holy Spirit. I was forever changed." Another minister said, "After being filled with the Holy Spirit, I wept for three days. My life was transformed." Both of these men became prayer warriors and mighty men of God.

The baptism in the Holy Spirit often brings with it weeping and holy laughter. Both are forms of self-travail. This travail from the innermost part of one's being can include contractions of the stomach muscles, *"groanings"* (see Romans 8:26) and even screaming (see the following chapter). Anointed screaming, a loud crying from deep within, releases the emotional poisons of bitterness and other hurts in our lives. It is often an important part of life-changing self-travail.

Deep laughter in the Spirit is also a form of self-travail that can lead to deep inner healing. Also, such laughter frequently triggers deep sobbing or crying. These manifestations of the Spirit are powerful in releasing us from the hurts of the past and in inner cleansing.

Speaking in Tongues for Three Days

A lovely saint of God received the baptism in the Holy Spirit in about 1910. "For three days I could speak no words in English, only in tongues. The presence of God was upon me the whole time. The Lord did such a deep work of inner transformation in my life. I became a new person." This woman became deep in prayer, faith and inner holiness, and from her family line came a number of outstanding men and women of God, one of whom ministered in more than eighty nations of the world, and another who ministered in more than a hundred and fifty nations of the world.

DEEPLY BAPTIZED IN THE HOLY SPIRIT

As you hunger for more of God, you can be refilled with the Holy Spirit and receive a greater anointing in your life too. Jesus promised:

Blessed are they which do hunger and thirst after righteousness: for they shall be filled. Matthew 5:6

Blessed are ye that hunger now: for ye shall be filled.
Luke 6:21

How can your hunger for the Lord be made to grow? Here are some steps you can take to increase your hunger for Him.

Make more time for Him, giving priority to the things of the Spirit. For instance, give up some of your favorite television time. Give up certain magazines or hobbies. Get up thirty minutes earlier in the morning to seek Him. Pray at least thirty minutes a day in tongues and study the Word of God.

Each of us needs to be deeply baptized in the Holy Spirit and to have rivers of living water flowing from deep within us. Sing in tongues. Praise and worship in tongues. Intercede and do spiritual warfare in tongues. Let the *"rivers"* flow out through you. Your hunger will quickly grow, and your life will be transformed, for Jesus declared:

> *He that believeth on me, as the scripture hath said, out of his belly shall flow rivers of living water. (But this spake he of the Spirit, which they that believe on him should receive: for the Holy Ghost was not yet given; because that Jesus was not yet glorified.)*
>
> John 7:38-39

THE KEY TO LIFE-CHANGING INNER HEALING

Whenever I minister inner healing to individuals who do not speak in tongues, with their permission, I pray for them to speak fluently in tongues, usually in three or more unknown tongues. We all need to have great freedom in speaking in other tongues. This fluency, or ease, in speaking in tongues opens our spirits to the deep sanctifying work of the Holy Spirit. It then becomes much easier for us to open up to self-travail, and such

> *As you hunger for more of God, you can be refilled with the Holy Spirit and receive a greater anointing in your life too!*

self-travail is normally essential to life-transforming, quick inner healing.

Because many who are baptized in the Holy Spirit have shallow experiences, those experiences are too often not accompanied by inner healing or deliverance. Most of us do far too little singing, praying and spiritual warfare in tongues. We need much more teaching in the Body of Christ on the life-changing importance of regularly praying in tongues.

Deep or Shallow?

If any of the following conditions exist in your life, your experience in the Holy Spirit probably has not been deep enough, and you need to seek God more fully:

1. **You still have difficulty speaking easily or deeply in tongues, or you always whisper or speak quietly in tongues.**

In this case, you may be fearful that, at times, you are making the words up. Such doubt and unbelief keep your experience shallow. Fear not! Here is some life-changing good news: Your tongues are always from the Spirit and never from the flesh. Jesus said:

> *If a son shall ask bread of any of you that is a father, will he give him a stone? or if he ask a fish, will he for a fish give him a serpent? Or if he shall ask an egg, will he offer him a scorpion? If ye then, being evil,*

know how to give good gifts unto your children: how much more shall your heavenly Father give the Holy Spirit to them that ask him? Luke 11:11-13

Confess this truth over and over again, that you are getting bread and not a stone, a fish and not a serpent. You will soon gain the revelation that your speaking or singing in tongues is always from the Lord, and you are never making it up. This truth will bring a wonderful change in your prayer life, and it will free you to speak much more deeply in tongues.

2. **You have never spoken in more than one or two languages in tongues.**

The Word of God refers to *"divers kinds of tongues"* (1 Corinthians 12:10) or *"diversities of tongues"* (1 Corinthians 12:28), which simply means "many" and "varied." Countless thousands of Spirit-filled Christians, including Pattie and me, speak in many unknown tongues, and this blesses our lives greatly.

God has this experience for you also. By faith, start speaking in a different language, then another new one, until you have spoken in four or five new tongues. Speaking a new language in tongues will be like shifting from first to second gear. Then the next new tongue will be like shifting into third gear. By the third or fourth tongue, you will be in overdrive! Isn't that exciting?

Never stop growing and deepening your experience. Go ahead and speak in four or five more languages now.

FREE FROM THE PAST

Remember that you will always get bread and not a stone, a fish and not a serpent. Your language will not be made up or copied. It will be from God. His Word promises you this. Always stand on what His Word, His truth, declares, not on your feelings about His truth.

> *Shouting in tongues, even for a few minutes, will often cause inner healing or deliverance from evil spirits to begin!*

3. You haven't felt a strong desire to pray in tongues, to read the Bible or to go to Spirit-led meetings.

These are all sure indications that your experience in the Holy Spirit has not been deep enough. When you have a deep infilling of the Holy Spirit, a much deeper desire for the things of the Spirit will come into your life as a result.

What Can You Do to Receive a Greater Infilling of the Holy Spirit?

If you are already filled with the Holy Spirit, to deepen your experience, do the following:

1. For three days, shout loudly for thirty minutes in tongues each day.

The Baptism in the Holy Spirit and Inner Healing

This will help to release suppressed emotions and bring new joy, and the gifts of the Spirit will often begin to flow more freely in your life.

Is shouting scriptural? Yes, it is:

And it came to pass, when the people heard the sound of the trumpet, and the people SHOUTED WITH A GREAT SHOUT, that the wall fell down flat, so that the people went up into the city, every man straight before him, and they took the city.
Joshua 6:20 (Emphasis added)

And when the ark of the covenant of the LORD came into the camp, all Israel SHOUTED WITH A GREAT SHOUT, so that the earth rang again.
1 Samuel 4:5 (Emphasis Added)

Shouting in tongues, even for a few minutes, will often cause inner healing or deliverance from evil spirits to begin. You will be amazed and excited about what the Lord will do for you through shouting in tongues. He surely takes the *"foolish things of the world to confound the wise."* Try it.

Every day, when I am driving my car, I pray fervently in tongues. I shout or groan in travail and self-travail and even laugh in the Spirit. This practice has profoundly changed my life. Try this a few times in your automobile, and see what the Lord will do for you.

2. Pray or sing in tongues for twenty to thirty minutes every day.

FREE FROM THE PAST

Your intimacy with God will become greater. Your prayers will be answered more quickly. Your anointing in the Holy Spirit will grow and grow. The more you pray in tongues, the more you will enjoy it.

3. **When you pray or sing in tongues, be aware that you are praying or singing to Jesus.**

As you speak in tongues, be aware of the Lord's presence and even picture Him in front of you. This will enlarge your prayer life and intimacy with God.

As you do this, you often will begin to see Him in vision, even with your eyes open. Even at this moment, as you are reading this book, see Him before you. Look at Him. It may seem like imagination, but it is from the Lord. Keep practicing looking at Him, and your vision will become clearer. You will be greatly blessed as you open to this truth.

4. **By faith, change from one language in tongues to another.**

You will get bread and not a stone, a fish and not a serpent. You can do it, and it will deepen your prayer life greatly. Do it now!

5. **In all of this, seek more inner healing.**

The Conclusion

Being baptized in the Holy Spirit deeply not only

The Baptism in the Holy Spirit and Inner Healing

brings more power, joy and a great love for Jesus into our lives, but it also enables us to receive inner healing more easily. With a deep infilling of the Holy Spirit, you will have taken an important step in becoming *Free from the Past.*

Chapter 3

Inner Healing through Self-Travail

Therefore are my loins filled with pain: pangs have taken hold upon me, as the pangs of a woman that travaileth. Isaiah 21:3

Likewise the Spirit also helpeth OUR infirmities: for

FREE FROM THE PAST

we know not what we should pray for as we ought: but the Spirit itself maketh intercession for us with groanings which cannot be uttered. Romans 8:26

Blessed are they that mourn: for they shall be comforted. Matthew 5:4

SUE: ONLY A MIRACLE FROM GOD COULD MEND HER LIFE

> *Many of us are just as crippled as Sue was!*

Sue's mother didn't want her, and her abusive, alcoholic father was seldom home. "From childhood I had been burning with resentment toward my parents. I have to admit that I hated men and trusted no one.

"To make things incredibly worse, I was injured in a dreadful auto accident at the age of fifteen, and since then no one could even lightly touch my back. As a result, I was unable to participate in most sports, and had a lousy social life. I attended Brother and Sister Chappell's revival meeting [in Australia]. All I could do was limp forward for prayer, hoping God would heal my aching back," Sue said.

The Lord revealed to me, through the word of knowledge, that unforgiveness and bitterness from her painful childhood rejection and hurts were blocking Sue's physical healing. This had also opened the door for Satan to bring that horrible auto accident into her life. These words of knowledge touched her heart deeply. Then God did a great work within her.

She later described how it felt. "The power of God, like electricity, went through my body. What an awesome experience it was!" She crumpled into a heap on the floor, God's operating table, and for about forty-five minutes, she remained there travailing (sobbing) for herself in the Spirit until God's spiritual and physical operation was finished.

When Sue got up from the floor, she was a new person. A smile and the glory of God lit up her face, replacing the painful and weary look she had borne much too long. She had forgiven her mom and dad, and her former resentment was now replaced by a love for them.

She was also healed and pain-free. The Holy Spirit had healed both her spiritual ailments and her physical ailments. She could now look forward to a new life — sports, marriage and children. Even more importantly, she had a new, intimate relationship with the Lord Jesus.

Many of us are just as crippled as Sue was. If this has been true of you, through inner healing you, too, can be set free to fulfill God's plans and purposes for your life.

DOROTHY: SET FREE TO LOVE AND BE LOVED

At the age of about twenty, Dorothy was viciously raped. During the thirty years that ensued, this tragedy destroyed two marriages and damaged her relationships

FREE FROM THE PAST

with her children and friends. It filled Dorothy with bitterness, rage and shame, and her life was shipwrecked as a result.

When Dorothy cautiously approached me at the end of my morning teaching session at a Pentecostal campmeeting, she related the torment and the shame she had been carrying for years. She whispered to me, "Can you help me? I'm desperate. I can't go on living like this."

I replied, "Yes, Dorothy, I can if you will do what I tell you." Then I asked her, "Do you trust the Lord to work through me?"

She quickly answered, "Yes."

I continued, "Then raise your hands, and when I touch your head, I want you to do something that may seem strange, and even unspiritual. I want you to begin laughing at the tragedy of having been raped!" In the very next chapter, we will deal with the healing power to be found in holy laughter. It is awesome. I was sure holy laughter could produce a deep emotional healing within this woman.

Dorothy was a little stunned by my very unusual spiritual advice, but in childlike simplicity, she agreed to give it a try. When I touched her head, she forced herself to begin laughing at this horror in her life. Then the anointing of holy laughter came heavily upon her. After a while the travailing laughter changed to sobs from deep within her being. The sobbing, sometimes mixed with laughter, continued for about thirty minutes.

Before we had begun praying, Dorothy had been unable to forgive the rapist and unable to accept herself. But the bitterness, unforgiveness, fears and shame within her had now disappeared. At last, she was free from the pain and shame of that terrible experience of thirty years before. She was free to lead a normal life—to love and to be loved.

Like Dorothy, many of us need inner healing, to be set free from crippling hurts within. Jesus has made provision for your emotional and physical healing. Self-travail is a powerful key to such healing—whether in holy travailing laughter, anointed sobbing or a mixture of the two.

TIM: HUNDREDS OF PRAYERS BUT NO RESULTS!

"I've had hundreds of people pray about my back over a fifteen-year period," declared Tim, "and this is the first healing I've had in all that time. My back is completely healed. I have no more pain. I am seeing fruit in many other areas of my life as well."

Like many other men, Tim had been filled with rage and suppressed emotions due to painful emotional scars inflicted by his father in childhood. I encouraged him to cooperate with the Holy Spirit by shouting in tongues for the release of his emotions and of the rage he felt inside. He did this and was then able to open up to holy laughter. This, in turn, triggered a deep sobbing travail within him.

"Brother and Sister Chappell ministered to me on several different occasions," said Tim, "and because of this, I was able to forgive and release my inner rage toward my father and others. A new peace and joy came into my life, and I also fell in love with my wife again." Tim was a new person, all because he learned to travail before God for the emotional pain in his life.

Like Sue, Dorothy and Tim, you, too, can be set free from the past through travailing prayer and deep forgiveness of those who have hurt you. What are you waiting for? Why not do it right now?

The Power of Travailing Prayer

Through travailing prayer, we can powerfully intercede for the unsaved, for other Christians, for government leaders or even for entire nations. Such intercession involves spiritual warfare and the birthing of miracles. Self-travail, the travailing for one's own rejection, hurts, sins or other needs, is the key to rapid, life-transforming inner healing and deliverance—the work of inner sanctification. Such travail is not a cry of self-pity but an opening of inner wounds, to let the poisons of abuse, bitterness and rejection out, so that we can be set free and be healed.

Both travail and self-travail include sobbing (with or without tears), groanings, loud crying, anointed screams (get your pillow ready) and deep holy laughter. It usually comes upon believers when the Holy Spirit chooses. However, the Holy Spirit wants us, by faith, to cooperate with Him and allow Him to bring travail and self-travail upon us with greater frequency.

Inner Healing through Self-Travail

The Azusa Street Revival

The great Azusa Street revival of 1906 in Los Angeles was the beginning of the outpouring of the Pentecostal experience in America—the experience of the baptism in the Holy Spirit and speaking in other tongues. For the next fifty years or so, the inner work of sanctification was emphasized among Spirit-filled people. In church meetings and home prayer meetings, long periods were given to weeping in repentance for uncleanness, bad attitudes and other sins, both before and after being filled with the Holy Spirit. During these times of weeping, an important form of self-travail, much inner healing and cleansing took place. The result was dramatically changed lives and the manifestation of great holiness and miracle-working power. We clearly need more of this today.

> *Through travailing prayer, we can powerfully intercede for the unsaved, for other Christians, for government leaders or even for entire nations!*

Sister Edith Ward Heflin, a pioneer of faith, described to us how her husband, Wallace, Sr., would lie on the floor by his bed, crying out in loud, agonizing travail for souls. Since then, I have often heard other individuals cry out in this way when they were in deep travail for the salvation of others. I have also read of many sinners, in the revivals of George Whitefield, Charles Finney and others, crying out under the conviction of sin. Travail and self-travail is a ministry of the Holy Ghost, and it produces miracles in our lives.

The Conclusion

In the following chapters we will see many others, like Sue, Dorothy and Tim, who were set free from deep emotional wounds through self-travail (travailing for their own needs). This is God's dynamic inner healing tool. After applying these simple principles they were able to become the loving, joyous persons God had created them to be—free to love and be loved—to be givers and not takers. Each of them testified to walking in a new closeness with the Lord Jesus.

You, too, can be released from all hurts and pains from the past, and can become an instrument for setting others free. You can become the person God created you to be. Jesus wants to free you to be able to give and receive love and to enjoy greatly improved relationships with family members, friends and co-workers, and with God Himself.

Try it now! You can be *Free from the Past*—free to be the real you.

FREE FROM THE PAST

At destruction and famine thou shalt laugh. Job 5:22

ELIZABETH: SET FREE BY HOLY LAUGHTER

Elizabeth, a young Irish sister said, "I was strongly advised by my doctor not to come to your meeting. But I knew I was close to a nervous breakdown and was desperate for a miracle, so I not only attended; I went forward for prayer. I was so surprised when you prayed for me to laugh at my deep-seated childhood hurts."

Elizabeth did not cry or sob. She just laughed and laughed and laughed. She continued laughing for an entire hour. As a result, her whole countenance changed. She was smiling and relaxed and radiated peace because of the inner healing she had experienced through holy laughter.

She said, "I was set free from my childhood hurts, from much buried rage and from my frayed nerves—truly a great miracle from our Lord. To our wonderful God be the glory!"

RALPH: REJECTED BY FATHER AND MOTHER

Ralph was tall, thin and very tense. "I knew I was full of rage and childhood hurts. My early years had been ones of rejection by both my father and mother. As they [Brother and Sister Chappell] laid hands on me to laugh at those childhood emotional wounds, I instantly began laughing and crying at the same time." At times Ralph stopped laughing, and we prayed for him to continue, and he did. This went on for an hour or more.

CHAPTER 4

INNER HEALING THROUGH HOLY LAUGHTER

A merry heart doeth good like a medicine.
                                    Proverbs 17:22

And Sarah said, God hath made me to laugh, so that all that hear will laugh with me.   Genesis 21:6

Later, Ralph said, "I felt like a thousand volts of electricity were zapping through my body as I laughed and cried in the Spirit." The holy laughter pulled out the "stopper" from his container of childhood bitterness and rejection, and the pain poured out like water. The Scriptures warn:

> *Looking diligently lest any man fail of the grace of God; lest any root of bitterness springing up trouble you, and thereby many be defile.* Hebrews 12:15

The dangerous root of bitterness was removed from Ralph, and he was able to forgive his parents deeply for the first time. Tension, that had built up over many years, left him, and a deep peace came into his life. Our God is truly able to deliver! Ralph's life was forever changed.

> *The holy laughter pulled out the "stopper" from his container of childhood bitterness and rejection, and the pain poured out like water!*

MICHAEL: PAINED FROM HIS PARENTS' DIVORCE

Twelve-year-old, curly-headed Michael was in deep emotional pain from parental rejection and the pains of his parents' divorce. When I laid hands on him and directed him to "laugh," he fully cooperated and began laughing deeply in the Spirit at the tragedies in his life. His mother later wrote about what happened:

> "My son, Michael, had a mighty touch from the Lord. For two hours straight he laughed and cried his way to freedom from the terrible hurts he received when his father left home, and then again he had another good dose of Holy Ghost laughter the last night, being set free from the pains I had caused and the hatred of his brother through jealousy. ... Now he's a different boy, and we are close. He is no longer a rejected boy who can't socialize. His grades are improving. He now speaks with love of his father and can remember the good times. There is a compassion in him that is far beyond his years."

The son was not the only one to be set free. His mother continued:

> "God also set me free. I went forward and cried and screamed my way to freedom. Praise God!"

How Did the Laughter Begin?

You may wonder how holy laughter came so easily to Elizabeth, Ralph and Michael. Did it come spontaneously from the Lord? No, it came from the Lord, but by faith, as each of them willingly followed the directions of the Holy Spirit.

We let them know that holy laughter would produce deep inner healing. We had them pray loudly in tongues, and then we laid hands on them and told them to stop tongues and, by faith, to begin to laugh for their hurts and other emotional pains. They were obedient, and holy laughter flowed forth, and amazing healing took place.

It is just that simple! It works because it is not man's method but that of the Holy Spirit. You can do it now for the hurts, rejection and woundings in *your* life. Go ahead. Give it a try. Close your eyes and start laughing about the worst hurt in your life—and then about another hurt and another. You will be surprised what it will do for you.

Rodney Howard-Browne and the "Laughter" Revival

In April of 1989, while South African Evangelist Rodney Howard-Browne was conducting a meeting in upstate New York, holy laughter broke out among the people attending. This manifestation of holy laughter quickly spread until great numbers of laypeople, pastors, evangelists and other Christian leaders were affected. The meetings were spiritually fruitful. Large numbers of souls were won to the Lord, and backsliders returned to the Lord in droves.

By 1995, through this ministry, holy laughter had made its way into congregations all over America and into many foreign nations as well. As Rodney Howard-

Browne laid his hands on Christian leaders, this special anointing, by faith, was imparted to them, and they took it back with them to their own places of ministry. By 1997, the phenomenon had reached worldwide proportions. Now thousands of Christian leaders and multiplied thousands of Christian laypeople have had their lives transformed by this unusual outpouring of the Spirit.

> *Thousands of Christian leaders and multiplied thousands of Christian laypeople have had their lives transformed by this unusual outpouring of the Spirit!*

WHY IS GOD USING HOLY LAUGHTER TO BRING REVIVAL?

Many people question why God would use laughter to bring revival. The most important reason is that it produces inner healing, and with the healing comes an inner holiness and a more intimate relationship with God. Holy laughter also frequently triggers, or releases, deep sobbing or crying (self-travail), which is even more powerful in releasing God's people from the hurts of the past.

All over the world, God's Spirit is leading individuals into an intimate relationship with Him. He desires a deep inner work of transformation, and He is looking for those whom He can conform to the image of His Son.

Because of a special anointing upon his life, the holy laughter we are witnessing in Rodney Howard-Browne's meetings (and now in many other meetings, as well) comes spontaneously. It is unplanned and is not a result of man's efforts or methods.

Holy Laughter by Faith

Almost every manifestation of the Spirit that comes spontaneously, however, can also come by an act of faith. Other manifestations in this same category include dancing in the Spirit and speaking in tongues. As you step out in faith and begin worshipping or praising the Lord in the dance, God's anointing will be upon it. Whenever you speak or sing in tongues by faith, God will anoint it. It will always be from Him.

In the same way, as you begin to laugh in obedience to the promptings of the Spirit, what you are doing will be "in the Spirit" and not in the flesh. It will be "holy" laughter. You will receive *"bread"* and not *"a stone," "fish"* and not *"a serpent"* (Luke 11:11-12). The Holy Spirit won't force you to laugh. So you must begin by faith. It will be from God, and the blessings from it will change your life.

Our Inner Healing Ministry to the Irish in 1976

History reveals that over a period of several hundred

years the rulers of England cruelly persecuted the Irish. This caused the hearts of the Irish to become bitter and hardened. They were unable to cry, or sob, for their childhood hurts—the key to deep inner healing.

What could I do to help them? The Holy Spirit unfolded the answer. He revealed that if I could get the emotionally wounded Irish, in simple childlike faith, to open up to holy laughter for their hurts, their lives would be transformed.

But how could I get them to receive this manifestation of the Holy Spirit? Didn't it come only spontaneously? The Holy Spirit taught me that such laughter could also come by faith, and the Lord instructed me to:

1. Have individuals pray loudly in tongues.
2. Lay hands on their heads, and instruct them to instantly stop speaking in tongues and, by faith, to start laughing.

As I ministered to the Irish people in this manner, in the mighty name of Jesus, one person after another burst into holy laughter. I discovered, to my amazement, that after a few moments of such laughter, most individuals began to experience self-travail, sobbing and crying deeply for the hurts in their lives. Often holy laughter and crying were mixed together. It was a glorious time of God's anointing falling heavily upon the Irish people, and one life after another was transformed.

The inability of the Irish to cry or to sob had been overcome by the Holy Spirit's manifestation of holy laughter. We must all learn to open up to this blessing by faith. It's easy. It will work for you, and your life will be transformed too.

Laughter and Its Impact on Our Ministry

Holy laughter has become a major Holy Spirit "tool," or method, we use to set thousands of people free from deep rejection, anger, self-hatred and hurts of the past. Holy laughter is also a tool of spiritual warfare. I laugh at my trials, at my disappointments and even at Satan, for it brings me a deep certainty in my soul that Christ has made me *"more than a conqueror"* over all the things that would try to hinder me. This has opened me up to new dimensions in prayer, enabling me to receive deep inner healing and deliverance that I had never been able to receive before. I can now open up much more deeply to crying, groaning and sobbing before the Lord. And holy laughter can do the same for you.

As noted, the Bible states, *"A merry heart doeth good like a medicine"* (Proverbs 17:22). Our Bible is full of scriptures on joy, on rejoicing, on praising, on clapping our hands and even on dancing, for there are great blessings that come into our lives through joy. Joy is medicine to our bodies, to our emotions, to our minds and to our relationships. God's Word tells us:

> *For the kingdom of God is not meat and drink; but righteousness, and peace, and joy in the Holy Ghost.*
> Romans 14:17

FREE FROM THE PAST

Laughing at Trials

The most important time to laugh (or praise God) is when we don't want to, when circumstances are screaming at us to be negative. Our cash flow is low. Our bills are overdue. We have lost our job. Our spouse has just left us for someone else. At such times, we must laugh at the circumstances and praise God for the victory. Laughter is a language of faith, a language of victory and a language of joy.

God Commands Laughter

One day Job seemed to be having a very bad day. The Sabeans stole all his oxen and asses and slew all the servants who guarded them except one. Then lightning came from Heaven and burned up his sheep. After that, the Chaldeans stole his camels. A windstorm came upon the house where all his children were gathered for a party, and they were all killed. Not long afterward, Satan struck Job with painful boils all over his body.

Job had lost his children, his health and his wealth. So what advice did the Lord give him? He didn't tell Job to pray, to fast, or even to trust Him, but He did give Job a key to victory that is valid for all of us today. The Holy Spirit said to Job through one of his friends, *"At destruction and famine thou shalt laugh"* (Job 5:22). God was saying to Job (and to us) that we must laugh in faith at the tragedies in our lives. We must get rid of our self-pity and anger and trust Him to bring us into victory.

God knew that the quickest way for Job to move out of self-pity and depression into faith would be to begin laughing at his trials. Likewise, when you will be obedient to laugh when you don't want to, God will perform miracles for you. Your laughing will quickly bring joy and victory into your life.

Pattie and I Laughed Over Our Destroyed Vehicle

Some years ago a Christian friend repaired about twenty-five problem areas on our lovely, white, four-door Toyota. This included work on the transmission, an engine tune-up, extensive brake work, rust spots removed from the body, the cassette recorder repaired and even our broken radio antenna replaced. We were getting our vehicle into shape for a journey from Los Angeles, California, to Richmond, Virginia.

Not long after everything was fixed, I drove over to Glendale one day to do some shopping. I took

> *The most important time to laugh (or praise God) is when we don't want to, when circumstances are screaming at us to be negative!*

the Central-Brand exit into Glendale and waited patiently for the red light at Brand to change to green. I was beginning to make a left turn onto Brand when it seemed that lightning had struck. A young businessman sped through the red light and smashed into our car, leaving it a total loss.

Because the car was an older model, the insurance settlement we received was less than half of what it would cost to replace the vehicle. In spite of much resistance inside of me, with Pattie's encouragement, I laughed and laughed at the accident and praised God for the trial.

I certainly wasn't happy that our car was destroyed. I was laughing because I believed God would bring good out of the accident. I kept laughing and praising God until I felt a release of victory. I was believing that God would give us a better car.

ALL THINGS WORK TOGETHER FOR GOOD

I have experienced over and over in my life that the promise of God is true:

> *And we know that all things work together for good to them that love God, to them who are the called according to his purpose.*   Romans 8:28

In His perfect timing, following that trial of our faith, God guided us, and we were able to replace our Toyota with a much newer and finer car—a Pontiac Bonneville

SSE. It had a near-perfect beige leather interior and a brilliant, gold-colored exterior. Although it was used, it looked like a new car—inside and out. What a great miracle! We were so grateful to God for His provision.

Holy laughter works. It gets rid of fear and unbelief and produces faith.

When we submit to God, even in the trials of life, all things do work together for our good, and one way of proving our submission to Him is through exhibiting an attitude of praise and laughter.

God is continuing to bring miracle after miracle into my life—as I continue, in faith, to laugh and praise Him for my trials, and to thank Him for my miracles before I see them with my physical eyes. When we *"walk by faith, not by sight,"* He is pleased (2 Corinthians 5:7).

Therefore, let us laugh our way through every trial, and learn to live in the provision, peace and joy of the Lord.

"Priming the Pump" for the Waters of Holy Laughter to Flow

Can you laugh when you don't feel like laughing? Can you force laughter to come, and will it be in the Spirit? Absolutely! How do you do this? How can you begin laughing in the Spirit? The answer is "by priming the pump."

I'm a city person, but my father was from the country. They had hand pumps in those days, and they kept a small tin cup beside the pump to prime it. A small amount of water had to be poured into the pump to give it suction, then the handle was worked up and down a few times, and soon water was gushing out in a great stream.

There is a "priming of the pump" that applies in many spiritual areas. Most of us have probably done this, even if we didn't know about this spiritual principle. We have all learned to praise the Lord when we didn't feel like it or want to do it. And, as we compelled ourselves to praise God, the anointing came upon us, the presence of God increased, and we began to feel better and better. We were priming the pump.

We can do the same thing by jumping or leaping in the Spirit. The Bible says:

> *Blessed are ye, when men shall hate you ... and cast out your name as evil, for the Son of man's sake. REJOICE YE IN THAT DAY, AND LEAP FOR JOY.*
>
> Luke 6:22-23 (Emphasis added)

When we are persecuted, disappointed, hurt or rejected, we must often force ourselves to praise the Lord. We trust Him to know what is best for us, and we make a decision to praise Him, even when our flesh is fighting

> *There is a "priming of the pump" that applies in many spiritual areas!*

the idea. This is what we mean by "priming the pump," and it works because God always anoints what He commands us to do.

Begin to force yourself to laugh at the pains of life—a laughter of faith. This will release you from anger, hurts, fears and self-pity and bring you into a place of joy and faith.

"Hee, Hee! Ha, Ha! Ho, Ho!"

Some twenty-one years ago the Lord revealed to me another awesomely important way to prime the pump in order to receive holy laughter. As I reveal this simple, yet life-changing, truth to you, keep in mind the Scriptures teach:

> *God hath chosen the foolish things of the world to confound the wise; and God hath chosen the weak things of the world to confound the things which are mighty.*
> 1 Corinthians 1:27

The Lord revealed to me that I should have individuals focus on their emotional pain, pray loudly in tongues, and then say, "Hee, hee! Ha, ha! Ho, ho!" several times. As they were obedient to the Lord and did this, holy laughter was triggered, deep inner healing was experienced, and lives were profoundly changed.

The Lord Himself called this "the Hee-hee! Ha-ha! Ho-ho! revelation." I now use this Holy Spirit method extensively, and many lives are blessed by it. When used as the Holy Spirit directs, it produces amazing results.

You Can Do It

When you are feeling discouraged or have hurts that need healing, close your eyes, force yourself to raise your head, and then begin praising the Lord in tongues (or English) for a minute or two. Then begin saying, "Hee, hee! Ha, ha! Ho, ho!" and repeat it several times. If you cooperate with the Holy Spirit, this will usually release a flow of holy laughter.

If that doesn't work, try saying, "Ho! Ha! Hee, hee!" or "Ho, ho! Hee, hee! Ha, ha!" This is not being silly; it is being spiritual! God takes the *"foolish things of the world to confound the wise."* These words are holy words, heavily anointed by the Holy Spirit and amazingly effective. To the natural mind, this "method" is totally absurd and so ridiculous, but it will usually produce holy laughter in anyone who tries it. God's methods bear fruit.

If your spouse has just hurt you deeply, your child has just wrecked the automobile, and the insurance expired three days ago, raise your head and say, "Ha, ha!, husband (or wife); Ho, ho!, automobile; Hee, hee!, expired insurance." Soon the laughter will come. Try it. It works. Fear and unbelief will depart, and faith and joy will come.

Be childlike. Be humble. Laugh your way to victory! Would you like a wonderful blessing at this very moment? If so, get out a piece of paper and write down two or three of your worst trials, and then start laughing at them with your eyes closed. Use the "Hee, hees!" and the "Ha, ha's!" Yes, right now!

As you begin to laugh, force yourself to continue, and not to go back into English or tongues. Laugh, even if you think you are making it up. You are getting *"bread"* and not *"a stone," "a fish"* and not *"a serpent."* You will be priming the pump, and soon you will feel the laughter coming spontaneously.

Praising God for Trials

Praise God for trials. Laugh at them, count them all joy, and leap for joy because of them. When you do this, you are putting God in control of your life. Otherwise, people and circumstances will control your life and your emotions. As a result, you will live with a "victim" mentality instead of a "more-than-a-conqueror" mentality.

Don't condemn yourself for your past. You are not a victim ... unless you choose to be one. Regardless of your childhood, education or other negative circumstances, God has a plan of victory for you. He will bring good out of the tragedies in your life, so start laughing at them and receive, through this laughter (and the crying that may come with it), emotional healing from the past.

Even God Laughs

He that sitteth in the heavens shall laugh: the Lord shall have them in derision. Psalm 2:4

FREE FROM THE PAST

The Lord shall laugh at him: for he seeth that his day is coming.   Psalm 37:13

God laughs at principalities and powers, and He laughs at Satan himself. Our God knows that the victory is His, and He knows that we also have the victory, for it has been purchased for us through the shed blood of Jesus Christ. Paul wrote:

Now thanks be unto God, which always causeth us to triumph in Christ.   2 Corinthians 2:14

HOLY LAUGHTER RELEASES FORGIVENESS TOWARD OTHERS

Laughter will release forgiveness, rid you of bitterness and bring inner healing into your life. Holy laughter will help release deep forgiveness in your life so you can be free from the emotional pain of hurts and be free to live at a new level of love, joy and peace.

Pride—a fear of looking foolish in front of people and a fear of losing control—can easily hold you back from laughing. Religious tradition can cause you to believe laughter isn't necessary or even scriptural. But it will be worth it all if you just give it a try. You will know forgiveness is complete when the emotional pain is gone from the hurt or disappointment and has been replaced by a deep peace.

Holy laughter, sobbing and tears are powerful in re-

INNER HEALING THROUGH HOLY LAUGHTER

leasing unforgiveness and bitterness. Cooperate fully with the Holy Spirit and let Him do this for you.

As you learn more about inner healing for your own life, God will bring hurting people to you for ministry. In the same way, you can minister to them for laughter for the hurts in their lives, and God will bring mighty releases within them too.

"EXCEPT YE BECOME AS LITTLE CHILDREN"

As we have seen, God uses *"the foolish things of this world."* Jesus said:

> *Verily I say unto you, Except ye be converted, and become as little children, ye shall not enter into the kingdom of heaven.*
>
> Matthew 18:3

To enter the greatness of God's blessings, you must come to Him with a childlike simplicity, hunger and trust, putting down your pride and saying, "Here I am, Lord. Do whatever it takes to set me free. If I have to laugh, if I have to scream, if I have to dance or jump, Lord, I will do it. I must get set free. I

> *As you learn more about inner healing for your own life, God will bring hurting people to you for ministry!*

want all You have for my life. Here I am, Lord. Do what needs to be done. I'm willing to look foolish, for I'm determined to be set free." When you come with this attitude, you will be set free, you will be blessed greatly, and the glory of God will fill your life in a mighty way.

I don't know about you, but I am hungry to be continually changed, hungry to be closer to God, to know Him better, and to be a greater blessing to my family and to the family of God. I believe that's what you want too, and that's the reason you are reading this book.

The Conclusion

Holy laughter has been a great blessing in my life and in the lives of thousands of others, in enabling the Holy Spirit to change us on the inside, to bring new dimensions of sanctification within, through inner healing and deliverance. Through holy laughter, the Lord will do the same for you and, through you, for many others. So make a list of your hurts, broken dreams, destroyed relationships and other major disappointments and start laughing and laughing and laughing at them. God's desire is for you to be totally *Free from the Past*.

CHAPTER 5

INNER HEALING THROUGH FORGIVENESS

And grieve not the holy Spirit of God ... Let all bitterness, and wrath, and anger, and clamour, and evil speaking, be put away from you, with all malice: and be ye kind one to another, tenderhearted, forgiving one another, even as God for Christ's sake hath forgiven you.   Ephesians 4:30-32

FREE FROM THE PAST

Judge not, and ye shall not be judged: condemn not, and ye shall not be condemned: forgive, and ye shall be forgiven.   Luke 6:37

> *Unforgiveness carries with it a root of bitterness, which will eventually spring up and defile, or contaminate, our relationships!*

Unforgiveness carries with it a root of bitterness, which will eventually spring up and defile, or contaminate, our relationships—in marriage, with our children, our friends and others. It will also damage our relationship with God. It will open the door to sicknesses and financial curses. We must forgive and get free from all bitterness.

Walking in forgiveness, practicing forgiveness as a way of life and praying blessings on those who hurt you are keys to good physical, emotional and mental health.

SARAH: PARALYSIS HEALED THROUGH FORGIVENESS

A dentist had accidentally cut a nerve in Sarah's lower jaw, resulting in partial paralysis of her face. She came to Pattie and me for a healing prayer. "Are you willing to forgive the dentist," we asked.

She replied, "I know I must. Please help me to do it."

Later, she remembered, "They then led me in a prayer of forgiveness for that terrible mistake of the dentist. They even had me pray a prayer of blessing for him. When I did this, something released inside of me. All bitterness toward him evaporated."

We didn't even need to pray for the healing of her jaw. The paralysis left during the prayer of forgiveness and inner healing, and her jaw was totally healed. Forgiveness is powerful. It sets us free in many different areas of our lives.

Maggie: An Ulcer Caused by Bitterness Was Healed through Forgiveness

In our meetings in Australia a number of years ago, Maggie, age twenty-one, came forward desiring healing for a painful stomach ulcer. By a word of knowledge I spoke these words to her: "You were hurt deeply when you were thirteen, and your unforgiveness is the cause of your stomach ulcer!"

Maggie began to cry, and said, "Yes, someone hurt me terribly at that age, and I have held bitterness in my heart against him ever since. But I am willing to forgive." She repented of her bitterness, and, with many tears, forgave the offender. Again, we didn't need a healing prayer. As she forgave and allowed the Holy Spirit to remove the rage within and to heal her hurting heart, she was instantly healed. All the pain from the ulcer left.

FREE FROM THE PAST

THE PRINCIPLE OF SOWING AND REAPING

The Kingdom of God is based on sowing and reaping. The Bible says:

> *Be not deceived; God is not mocked: for whatsoever a man soweth, that shall he also reap. For he that soweth to his flesh shall of the flesh reap corruption.*
>
> Galatians 6:7

When we sow unforgiveness and the bitterness that comes from it, as Sarah and Maggie did, we will surely reap the curses that accompany it. When we sow good things, then we will reap blessings. When we deeply forgive, as Sarah and Maggie eventually did, blessings will flood into our lives. Miracles will take place. Relationships with others and with God will dramatically improve. So, what are we waiting for? Let us become forgiving, loving Christians.

JANE: HER PARENTS ARE SAVED

"For many years," said Jane, "I had been interceding for my parents' salvation, but they had made it clear that they wanted no part of my 'religion.' This rejection hurt me deeply." The Holy Spirit brought conviction to Jane that she had bitterness in her heart toward her parents because of their rejection of Christianity. We laid hands on her and ministered inner healing and repentance for this bitterness.

She later told us, "After weeping for a long time on my face before God, the emotional pain of rejection was gone. I no longer had any unforgiveness, only love, for my parents."

Later Jane gave us this amazing testimony, "Within five days, both of my parents were mightily saved." Jesus has commanded us to forgive and walk in love toward everyone. It is unforgiveness that is hindering many of our prayers.

MARY: HER ALCOHOLIC HUSBAND WAS SAVED

"For years my marriage had been a living hell because of my alcoholic husband," said Mary. "Even after fifteen years of hard prayer from me and others, my husband seemed further from the Lord than ever. Then one day the Holy Spirit convicted me of self-righteousness, self-pity, a judgmental attitude toward my husband and the sin of unforgiveness. I deeply repented of these sins and forgave my husband for the hurts and disappointments of our marriage."

Mary's husband now had a new wife, and soon she had a new husband, for within two weeks he was delivered from alcoholism, saved and filled with the Holy Ghost! Forgiveness is just that powerful.

WINNING OUR LOVED ONES

Many of us, like Jane and Mary, have been praying long and hard for an unsaved loved one. Often our loved ones have some terrible habits, attitudes, selfishness or sins in their lives that really hurt, frustrate or embarrass us. When we stand praying and believing for the miracle of salvation in their lives, we must forgive them completely.

Unforgiveness destroys or weakens our power to get loved ones saved. We must deeply forgive them in order to have the power to release them from the demonic darkness that blinds them to truth and holds them back from salvation.

What Forgiveness Is Not

In order to be able to forgive deeply, we need to understand what forgiveness is not:

1. Forgiveness is not weakness, but rather strength.
2. Forgiveness does not restore trust, but rather opens the door to the possibility of reestablishing such trust. Forgiveness is a free gift, but trust must be earned.
3. Forgiveness often does not include a restoration of a relationship, friendship or marriage. You must forgive your divorced or separated spouse, ex-prayer partner, ex-boss or ex-pastor, but the relationship often will not be restored.
4. Forgiveness is not condoning sin or saying that what was done was okay. If a person has sinned against you and/or God, he or she is guilty and

must answer to God. But He has said, *"Dearly beloved, avenge not yourselves, but rather give place unto wrath: for it is written, Vengeance is mine; I will repay, saith the Lord"* (Romans 12:19).

THEN, WHAT IS FORGIVENESS?

Forgiveness is releasing a person from a debt owed to us. We give up our right to get revenge for the wrong someone has done to us. We lose our desire to "get even."

In the Old Testament, some revenge was permitted, but only as mercy to avoid greater retribution. God allowed *"an eye for an eye, and a tooth for tooth,"* but no more (Matthew 5:38). He did not allow two eyes for one eye, or two teeth for one tooth.

> **Unforgiveness destroys or weakens our power to get loved ones saved!**

In the New Testament, the dispensation of grace, we are commanded to turn the other cheek, go the extra mile and actually bless our enemies. Jesus instructed us:

> *Love your enemies, bless them that curse you, do good to them that hate you, and pray for them which despitefully use you, and persecute you.*
>
> Matthew 5:44

FREE FROM THE PAST

If we can develop a lifestyle of praying blessings for those who hurt, disappoint and reject us, instead of criticizing and complaining, our lives will be dramatically blessed. We will live in new joy, peace and love.

OTHER REASONS TO FORGIVE

There are many other reasons to forgive. Here are some of them:

1. God will forgive us of our sins only when we forgive others. Jesus said, *"Judge not, and ye shall not be judged: condemn not, and ye shall not be condemned: forgive, and ye shall be forgiven"* (Luke 6:37).
2. Unforgiving people are hurting people, and they hurt others. Forgive deeply, and allow the Holy Spirit to bring healing to your hurting heart, and this act will free you from hurting others.
3. Unforgiveness weakens our prayer power, particularly for the person for whom we are praying. The Word of God tells us, *"And when ye stand praying, forgive, if ye have ought against any: that your Father also which is in heaven may forgive you your trespasses"* (Mark 11:25).
5. Unforgiveness can cause us to become sick. It can also keep us from being healed and prevent us from maintaining our healing.
6. Unforgiveness can cause or contribute to emotional (or mental) sickness.

7. Unforgiveness can cause financial curses.
8. When we fail to forgive, we will become like the person we criticize, judge or hold bitterness toward.
9. If we men fail to honor our wives (which includes forgiveness), our prayers will be hindered: *"Likewise, ye husbands, dwell with them according to knowledge, giving honor unto the wife, as unto the weaker vessel, and as being heirs together of the grace of life; that your prayers be not hindered"* (1 Peter 3:7).
10. Forgiveness of the one who has hurt us is an important key to our being released from negative soul ties (bondage) with them. It is also a key to the breaking of generational curses, particularly the deep forgiveness toward a mother or father.
11. We will never rise to greatness in God—greatness in ministry and greatness in relationships—until we forgive from our hearts those who have hurt us.

Hurts and Bitterness toward Parents

As we have seen, no matter how good we think our childhood was, we have vastly more hurts and rejections than we can imagine, and most of them often remain forgotten or buried. These hurts can cause us to distrust our marriage partner in various ways (as we see our parents' negative qualities in them). Our deep forgiveness of our parents sets us free to *"cleave"* to our mate, to truly know them, to trust them and to love them more deeply. Jesus stated:

FREE FROM THE PAST

> *For this cause shall a man leave father and mother, and shall cleave to his wife: and they twain shall be one flesh.*
>
> Matthew 19:5

Deep forgiveness of our mother and father frees us to "leave" our parents, ... and to "cleave" in perfect, godly unity to our mate!

Deep forgiveness of our mother and father frees us to *"leave"* our parents, to become free from negative dependence upon them, and to *"cleave"* in perfect, godly unity to our mate.

DINAH: A MARRIAGE IN TROUBLE

Dinah said, "I had repeated arguments and fights with my husband. I hated men. My marriage was about to break up when, in desperation, I came for help." As Pattie and I ministered to Dinah for inner healing, the Lord revealed to us that the root cause of her marital problem was bitterness toward her father. When I laid hands on her and prayed for the healing of the wounds from her father's rejection, she was slain under the power of God, and for about thirty minutes, she sobbed deeply in self-travail.

Later she told us, "What a miracle! I was now able to deeply forgive my father. This forgiveness of my father released the rage within toward other men, including my husband. I was amazed. I saw my husband in an entirely new light. I now loved him, and God gave us a new marriage."

PATRICIA: "I HATE MY HUSBAND"

Some years ago, while we were ministering in Australia, Patricia approached me, also in desperation, and whispered, "I hate my husband. I want to love him, but I can't stand him. Can you help me?"

Just as with Dinah, the Holy Spirit showed me that unforgiveness toward her father was the root cause of Patricia's hatred and distrust of her husband. "The problem is your father, Patricia," I said. "Are you willing to forgive him?"

She was surprised by this, but she replied, "Yes, I need help. My relationship with my father *was* terrible, and it's true, I do hate him."

Pattie and I began praying for her for a release from the terrible hurts and rejection from her father. She began sobbing deeply and "fell out" under the power of God onto the Lord's operating table.

She later related, "I travailed in deep sobbing for about thirty minutes. The rejection and hurts from my dad totally left, and my bitterness toward him was gone. I forgave him for the terrible childhood abuse, and now I actually felt a love for him."

FREE FROM THE PAST

As the hatred toward her father left, Patricia's hatred toward her husband also melted away and was replaced by love. The result was that the marriage was restored.

The Conclusion

Many of us have been deeply rejected or hurt by others. Our Lord calls us to forgive, even as He has forgiven us. Such deep forgiveness often can only come through our being healed from the rejection and hurts we have suffered at the hands of others. We must allow forgiveness and blessing of others, in word and deed and from the heart, to become a way of life. In so doing, we will sow a multitude of blessings into our own lives and into the lives of others.

You will be overjoyed at the effect this type of forgiveness will have on your relationships with others and with God. It will bring joy and peace into your life. In addition, it will be a big factor in your being healed physically and in keeping your healing. Try it. You, too, can be *Free from the Past*.

CHAPTER 6

BREAKING THE POWER OF GENERATIONAL INIQUITY

And the LORD passed by before him, and proclaimed, The LORD, The LORD God, merciful and gracious, longsuffering, and abundant in goodness and truth, keeping mercy for thousands, forgiving iniquity and transgression and sin, and that will by no means clear the guilty;

FREE FROM THE PAST

visiting the iniquity of the fathers upon the children, and upon the children's children, unto the third and to the fourth generation.   Exodus 34:6-7

MARTHA: DELIVERED FROM INHERITED SPIRITS

"I am desperate for ministry," said Martha. "For years I have been suffering from an ulcer, arthritis and neck pains. Can you help me?" She also was strongly oppressed by spirits of witchcraft, suicide, murder, fear of death, lust and insanity. All of these spirits were inherited from her family line. They were generational curses.

In her childhood, Martha's parents had rejected her. She had never been told she was loved, and this wounded her spirit deeply. This rejection provided an open door for evil spirits to have a strong influence in her life.

When we met Martha and saw her need, we felt a deep compassion for her. We wanted to see her set free. Through much spiritual warfare, we broke the power of the generational curse of witchcraft, lust and insanity on her life.

"As they ministered to me, for a long period of time," Martha later related, "I both laughed and sobbed in travail for the deep emotional wounds I had carried all of my life. I could tell as those spirits left me! I also knew the Lord was healing my emotions. All my fears and lust were gone. Wow! I felt so different."

God did a deep work of inner healing and deliverance in Martha that day, and her emotions became stable. Through the inner healing, she also was physically healed of ulcers, arthritis and her neck problem. What a great God we have! He does all things well. Thank You, Lord Jesus.

Phyllis: Freed from Occultic Bondage

Phyllis, age twenty-seven, stood tall and regal at five ten. "I have been afraid of men all my life and have never married," she said. "I have lustful dreams and thoughts. My emotions are so bottled up. Can you help me?"

Phyllis had experimented with transcendental meditation, and her grandmother and other family members had been involved in occultic practices. There was also sexual lust in the family line. These witchcraft spirits from her exposure to transcendental meditation made her fear and dislike of men greater and were the primary cause of her lustful dreams. She needed deliverance from these spirits and much inner healing.

> *What a great God we have! He does all things well!*

I broke the generational curse of occultism and lust with powerful spiritual warfare in the mighty name of Jesus. I also had her picture herself standing behind the cross and her parents in front of the cross. I had her see the generational curses of her family line stopping at the cross, and then see them placed on Jesus—who became a curse for us. You can do this also.

"As a child, my father had ignored me," she told us, "giving me little affection. It hurt me deeply. I got along poorly with Mom also. This caused a deep wounding in my heart. I have been so rejected all of my life."

Phyllis described later to me how this ministry to her had changed everything. "I can now cry before the Lord," she said, "and feel His presence deeply. The Lord has become my Friend. I am free of lustful dreams, and my fear of men is totally gone. I am able to make friends with others more easily."

VIRGINIA: HINDRANCES REMOVED

"I could only speak a few words in tongues, and I knew this limited my prayer life, as well as my relationship with the Lord," said Virginia. "Our whole family had been involved in the New Age movement, and I was still being harassed by those New Age evil spirits."

We prayed a strong prayer of deliverance over her, breaking the generational curse of witchcraft. We then commanded those spirits, in Jesus' name, to release her so she could speak freely in tongues.

Virginia later testified, "Something broke inside of me, and I found myself praying in tongues from deep within. I became so much more aware of the presence of the Lord. It was wonderful!"

Some Christians cannot pray freely in tongues because of an evil spirit blocking them. However, the more usual cause of being unable to pray in tongues fluently is because of the fear of making it up. Good news: It will never be made up. It will always be *"bread and not a stone, fish and not a serpent"* (Matthew 7:9-10). It is God's responsibly to make it real. Ours is just to speak it out!

One of the most important laws of the Kingdom of God is that whatever we sow we will reap (see Galatians 6:7). It is true either positively or negatively, for either bad or good. This principle works individually, as well as corporately. Even whole nations reap what has been sown. This principle applies to business corporations, labor unions, church denominations, individual churches and any other group. It is true also of families.

Through the sins of our "family line," we reap negatively (and positively, in generational blessings) what has been sown by previous generations. Most of our sins, demonic oppressions, lust, addictions, weaknesses, bad attitudes and failures in life have their root in a negative inheritance from our family line. The Bible states:

> *Keeping mercy for thousands, forgiving iniquity and transgression and sin, and that will by no means clear the guilty; visiting the iniquity of the fathers upon the children, and upon the children's children, unto the third and to the fourth generation.*   Exodus 34:7

> *Thou shalt not bow down thyself to them, nor serve them: for I the L<small>ORD</small> thy God am a jealous God, visiting the iniquity of the fathers upon the children unto the third and fourth generation of them that hate me.*   Exodus 20:5

FREE FROM THE PAST

It does seem unfair that we suffer the effects of sins committed by ancestors, but it is true nevertheless. The sins of our family line, going all the way back to the third and fourth generation, bring harmful occurrences and even curses into our lives.

> *In turn, we parents, through our sins, can bring curses upon our children and grandchildren!*

In turn, we parents, through our sins, can bring curses upon our children and grandchildren, and these can have an evil effect unto the third and fourth generation as well. As an example, when a mother has depression, her daughter will usually have depression. If a father or a mother has a strong spirit of lust, in most cases their children will have the same problem. Dishonest parents breed dishonest children.

In most cases these negative qualities go far back into the family line. For example, when dealing with a grossly immoral person, a dishonest person, a liar or an alcoholic, you will normally find parents, grandparents and great-grandparents with similar sins or weaknesses.

VICTORY THROUGH THE BLOOD OF JESUS

Many of us have been incorrectly taught that once we are saved, such generational sin can no longer negatively affect our lives, that it is "under the blood." It is true that Jesus has purchased, through His precious blood, a total plan of salvation for us, a plan that includes forgiveness of our sins, inner sanctification and healing of our bodies, emotions, minds and finances. It also includes deliverance from the harmful effects of generational iniquity. Christ has defeated Satan for us. Victory in every area of our lives has been provided for us through His blood poured out on the cross at Calvary. Paul wrote to the Galatians:

> *Christ hath redeemed us from the curse of the law, being made a curse for us.*   Galatians 3:13

But these blessings, although they are available to us, do not come automatically. We must learn, through the Word of God, how to receive (or appropriate) them. We must learn how to enforce the victory won at Calvary for us by Jesus through His shed blood. While we will never be free completely from our Adamic nature, God has a plan for setting us free from the negative results of generational iniquity—the root cause of most problems in our lives.

Generational Curses Resulting from Exposure to the Occult

When a family member has been involved in the occult realm, every generational sin becomes stronger, and every weakness becomes an open door for demonic oppressions. For this reason, this chapter will give great emphasis to the generational curse resulting from occultism.

The occult includes such things as astrology, ouija boards, tarot cards, séances, Masons and Eastern Star. Typical of strong curses that result from dabbling in these evils are lust, abuse of children, depression, alcoholism, dishonesty, continual illness, repeated miscarriages or barrenness, being accident-prone, a family history of marital problems, incest, fears and rebelliousness. Most of us have been far more harmed by such family involvement than we realize.

The word *occult* means "hidden, mysterious or concealed." In the spiritual realm, this word encompasses all non-Christian or ungodly methods of seeking to know that which is hidden—whether dealing with the past, the present or the future. Through Satan's counterfeits, such as astrology, fortune-telling and palm reading, individuals seek to bypass God to discover hidden things. In doing so, they contact the defiling kingdom of darkness, Satan's realm, and open themselves to great tragedy.

It is often in this way that demonic spirits and curses come into people's lives and into the lives of their family members. It happened to me, and it has happened to the majority of believers, but God has total victory for all of us—if we are willing to seek Him.

Occultism embraces all secret orders. Because my father was a member of the Masons, a curse came into my life, and it brought harm to me and my family. I had to engage in spiritual warfare many times before I felt my victory over it was complete.

The Word of God declares:

The secret things belong unto the LORD our God: but those things which are revealed belong unto us and to our children for ever, that we may do all the words of this law. Deuteronomy 29:29

God Himself desires to reveal to us everything we need to know about the past, the present and the future, and He strictly forbids our seeking such information by Satan's methods. The Lord sternly warns us:

And I will cut off witchcrafts out of thine hand; and thou shalt have no more soothsayers. Micah 5:12

There shall not be found among you any one that maketh his son or his daughter to pass through the fire, or that useth divination, or an observer of times, or an enchanter, or a witch, or a charmer, or a consulter with familiar spirits, or a wizard, or a necromancer. For all that do these things are an abomination unto the LORD. Deuteronomy 18:10-12

God has given to the Church the indwelling Holy Spirit to reveal hidden things to us. The Lord tells us:

The Spirit of truth ... will guide you into all truth ... and he will shew you things to come. John 16:13

My sheep hear my voice, and I know them, and they follow me. John 10:27

FREE FROM THE PAST

The occult also includes using evil spirits, consciously or unconsciously, to supernaturally change events. This would include putting curses or blessings on people—a practice commonly known as witchcraft, or sorcery. The word *witchcraft* is often used to mean the same as *occult*.

We must avoid all forms of the occult, including exposing ourselves to television programs that contain it. We must be particularly careful to screen what our children are looking at, including programs having to do with witches, demons, ghosts, vampires or violence. We must also be aware that rock music carries occultic spirits.

Focused and Fervent Prayers

To fight generational curses, your prayers must be pinpointed, or focused, in specific areas of exposure. Focused prayers get answers. This applies to each area of the occult you may have been in or been influenced by. For example, recently the Lord was having me do spiritual warfare in specific areas of the occult to which I had been exposed—my use of the ouija board and of the pendulum, water dowsing or witching, going once to a fortune-teller and dabbling in hypnotism. I had to pray hard and repent in each area separately, with much groaning in the Spirit (self-travail). In fact, you will usually need to pray several times in each area to get the complete release, the complete victory.

As I lay on my face before the Lord, He showed me much occultism from my mother's side of the family, as well as some from my father's side. As a result, I have prayed about this for long periods, with much spiritual warfare and self-travail, and have had great breakthroughs. Prayer is hard work, and we need to pray until we get the assurance in our spirit that we have the victory. This is known as "praying through."

Be sure you are specific in your prayers. If you know that your grandmother, your uncle and your great-grandfather were into the occult, then forgive each of them separately for this negative inheritance. Pray much in tongues and do self-travail until you know the forgiveness is real, not just mental. It is also important to repent for all your relatives involved in the occult, unto the third and fourth generation. This type of prayer is known as "identification repentance," a frequent Old Testament prayer method.

> *The occult also includes using evil spirits, consciously or unconsciously, to supernaturally change events!*

Next, in Jesus' name, you must break the power of the spirits affecting you from each of these family members. When possible, take family members one at a time, not as a group. Do this also for the generational curses in other areas, such as lust, alcoholism, depression and fear.

You must not ask God to make the devil leave. Rather, in Jesus' name, *you* must take authority over him and break his power. *You* must command him to leave. Jesus proclaimed:

FREE FROM THE PAST

And I will give unto THEE the keys of the kingdom of heaven: and whatsoever THOU shalt bind on earth shall be bound in heaven: and whatsoever THOU shalt loose on earth shall be loosed in heaven.
Matthew 16:19 (Emphasis Added)

James taught the early church:

Submit yourselves therefore to God. Resist the devil, and he will flee from you. James 4:7

Jesus has given you the authority to bind Satan and to break his power, so do it! Weak, religious or complaining prayers will not accomplish anything in this regard. Your prayers must be passionate, and they must be intense. As the Scriptures declare:

The effectual fervent prayer of a righteous man availeth much. James 5:16

GENERATIONAL BLESSINGS

It is easy to get so caught up in the importance of generational curses that we overlook generational blessings:

For I the LORD thy God am a jealous God, visiting the iniquity of the fathers upon the children unto the third and fourth generation of them that hate me, and shewing mercy unto thousands of them that love me and keep my commandments. Deuteronomy 5:9-10

Breaking the Power of Generational Iniquity

We inherit a vast number of blessings from our family members, including intelligence, musical talent, business ability, athletic talent, a strong and healthy body, mental and emotional stability and excellent moral and spiritual qualities. The call of God often runs in family lines. We must be grateful for the family line God has placed us into, grateful for our heritage. He placed us in our particular family line for one of two reasons, and often for both reasons:

1. To be blessed by the good inheritance from it. (Most of us have been saved through the prayers of one or more family members.)

2. For the healing of our family line. We are stewards of it and need to be faithful in bringing healing to the whole family.

How do we do this? We do it by breaking the power of generational curses in our line and by living a life that is sanctified and separated unto God. Thus, generational blessings will flow to our family line through our consecrated life.

My Own Generational Blessings

There were preachers on both sides of my family in generations past. My grandmother from Mother's side was a Christian, and I believe her prayers and the prayers of those preachers in my family line are the reason I am a Christian today. I believe it is because of their prayers that in 1962 God laid it upon the heart of a powerful intercessor (whom we had never met) to intercede for my family. After five years of intercession by this lady, we met her daughter supernaturally and were saved and filled with the Holy Spirit through her.

We should be continually grateful for the multitude of generational blessings from the Lord, including being made in His image. Also, we should pray for those in our family line who will come after us, including our children and grandchildren.

> *We should be continually grateful for the multitude of generational blessings from the Lord, including being made in His image!*

TEENAGE EXPERIMENTATION IN THE OCCULT

During the difficult, often reckless, teenage period, many become involved with various forms of the supernatural. Individuals from every age-group, including a large number of teenagers, have become involved in the occult through what is called the New Age movement. This movement involves transcendental meditation, psychic powers of various types (including ESP), astrology, séances, the use of crystals or crystal balls, Yoga, hypnosis, psychic healing (a counterfeit of divine healing), Science of the Mind and a belief in reincarnation. Quite a few teenagers even get involved in the horrors of Satanism, and this can result in extensive spiritual, emotional and even physical abuse.

As we noted in a previous chapter, the teen years are also a time of sexual experimentation, which leads to strong negative soul ties and transference of evil spirits, including occult spirits, from one sexual partner to the other.

There is a great need in the Body of Christ today for a deeper understanding of how to get Christians freed from this type of witchcraft involvement. God may be calling you to be part of the answer for this generation.

Continuing Freedom

Because of the great victory God had given me through deliverance from occultic spirits, I thought I was totally free. I was incredibly changed and blessed. I was to learn, however, that I was only partially delivered and needed further releases from the occultic exposure and other generational curses. As I received more and more from the Lord, I gained more freedom, more peace and a greater closeness to Jesus and to my loved ones.

Several years ago, as I was meditating on generational iniquity, the Lord revealed to me a surprising and immensely important truth: that even when we have had much deliverance from generational curses, the deliverance is rarely more than ten to twenty-five percent complete. Later the Lord expounded on this revelation and showed me that this ten to twenty-five percent principle applies in many other areas, including inner healing and deliverance from negative soul ties, from inner vows and from financial curses.

Whenever God reveals a truth, it is to bless us and to set us free—never to condemn us. If we will cooperate with the Holy Spirit, what sounds like bad news can become good news. The truth is that all of us have the need of much more inner healing and deliverance—much of it involving generational curses. Such curses are often the root cause of one or more big problems in our lives. God has a mighty provision for setting us free through the shed blood of Christ and by the power of the Holy Spirit.

Again, we all walk in much denial, and facing these truths can be painful. If we are willing, however, it can lead to beautiful changes in our lives. May each of us be willing to face the truth about our need for inner healing and much more inner sanctification. Those bad attitudes, the occasional curse word, the lustful thoughts, the unclean dreams ... let us look at them as the tip of the iceberg of much inner darkness. And keep in mind, again, that an important root of every weakness, every sin and every bad attitude is in our generational inheritance, combined with our own bad choices.

Wonderful new releases and victories are coming your way, but these victories are not automatic. You must know the truth, so that you can be set free. You can be liberated to face the future in a whole new dimension of fulfillment.

Satanic Appointments vs. Divine Appointments

When your parents have been involved in séances, astrology, tarot card reading or other forms of witchcraft, it opens the door for Satan to bring destruction into your life. It also brings the wrong people and negative circumstances into your life. The very person who will be a curse in your life will be drawn to you. Strange accidents will happen to you.

This is about to change completely. The Father has a plan of total victory for you. He has many divine appointments of His own with which to bless you, and others through you.

It may take many sessions of deep prayer with much warfare, and probably much self-travail, but the time will come when you will know that you have prayed through completely. The Lord will give you an assurance within, a deep peace, that you have obtained complete victory in a particular area.

The Open Doors to Your Soul

You may not think that your exposure to the occult has been sufficient to merit such drastic action in prayer. After all, you only played with the ouija board once or twice. You were only in one séance. Your interest in astrology and ESP was only passing. And you can't understand how you could have been affected by listening to rock music. When a door has been opened into your soul, however, evil spirits can enter until that door has been shut. No wonder such involvement causes serious problems in the areas of sexual lust, money and power!

Probably seventy-five percent or more of us have been directly exposed to the occult and have a great need for these doors to be closed. How can you close those doors? First, break the power of witchcraft in your family line through much spiritual warfare. Then, command, in Jesus' name, that those doors be closed, and again do much praying in tongues in spiritual warfare.

Pray with authority. The Lord will give you an assurance when the doors are completely closed. With your eyes closed, if you ask Him, the Holy Spirit will often show you by vision whether or not the doors are closed. Pray until you receive that assurance.

The Conclusion

As we have observed, the generational curse from occultism is only one of many areas of generational iniquity that need to be broken. We must also focus our spiritual warfare on other areas of generational iniquity, such as depression, alcoholism, lust, nervousness, abusiveness, dishonesty, divorce and poverty. We inherit numerous curses from our family line.

All such inherited curses should be dealt with individually, not as a group. For example, if your mother

Breaking the Power of Generational Iniquity

suffered much depression, you probably will be attacked in this area also.

Let's Have A Prayer Together Now:

As you pray, see the cross of Jesus (picture it) between you and your mother and dad and between you and your entire four generations. Then pray this prayer:

> Father God, in Jesus' name, we thank You that through the shed blood of Your Son Jesus every generational curse is legally stopped at the cross as we appropriate it by heart faith. We break the power of witchcraft, lust, poverty, fear, depression, negativity and every spirit of sickness. We thank You that in the powerful name of Jesus it is done. We have the victory. Every generational curse is stopped!
>
> Amen!

Probably seventy-five percent or more of us have been directly exposed to the occult and have a great need for these doors to be closed!

Alone with God, ask Him to reveal sins in your life that need to be repented of, including, lukewarmness, grumbling and complaining, unforgiveness, sexual sin and watching too much TV or the wrong kind of TV or movies. Let the Holy Spirit intercede for you, by praying in tongues. Sin opens the door for the curse of generational sins to remain in our lives. Close those doors.

Also, with tears, deeply forgive your parents for childhood rejection and other hurts. Deep forgiveness of parents through inner healing is the most important key to being released completely from generational curses.

God's will, and His great desire, is to set us totally free from every negative effect of generational iniquity. Learning just a few of the Holy Spirit methods in this chapter will benefit you immensely and enable you to be free and to help free others. Learn to use these powerful Holy Spirit methods, and you will be *Free from the Past.*

Chapter 7

Breaking the Power of Destructive Inner Vows

Swear not at all … . But let your communication be, Yea, yea; Nay, nay: for whatsoever is more than these cometh of evil. Matthew 5:34-37

This word *swear* means "to vow, to promise, to affirm, or to confess." Unless vows are inspired by the Holy

FREE FROM THE PAST

Spirit, they can produce great harm in our lives. Vows made in childhood, although often long forgotten, are the most harmful and often have far-reaching and devastating effects on individuals throughout their lives.

JANET: "I WILL NEVER LET MYSELF BE HURT AGAIN"

For most of our meeting, Janet sat expressionless, with a blank, hollow look on her face. She told us, "I was sexually abused as a child, rejected by my father and given little love by my mother. In childhood, I made a decision deep within my heart that I would never allow anyone to hurt me again."

Janet accomplished this by refusing to give or to receive love. As an adult, she found herself locked into a self-made prison, held in bondage by this inner vow not to be hurt, not to love and not to let people get to know her. Now thirty years old, Janet came to our meeting in desperation, feeling she could not go on living without an inner healing miracle from God.

> *Vows made in childhood, although often long forgotten, are the most harmful and often have far-reaching and devastating effects on individuals throughout their lives!*

"The pain within my heart has been overwhelming," she continued. "I have been unable to establish a close relationship with anyone. As a result, I have no real friends and have never married."

We explained to Janet that she would need to break the childhood inner vow. Although it had protected her from hurts for so many years, it was now destroying her. Her inner vow, which had been a wall of protection, had become instead a prison. Many people are in that same prison because of an inner vow made in their childhood, and you may be one of them. I was.

Breaking the Inner Vow and Coming Out of Prison

We asked Janet if she was willing to break the inner vow, and she said, "Oh, yes!"

We next asked her if she was willing to forgive her father, her mother and the sexual abuser. She quickly affirmed her willingness. "Yes, yes, yes!" she said, "I can't go on any longer as I am." She made the decision to become vulnerable, to begin to trust people again.

Next, we took her through a prayer of forgiveness and a long blessing prayer for her father, for her mother and then for the sexual abuser. We then proceeded, in the mighty name of Jesus, to have her do spiritual warfare in loud tongues and even in holy laughter. After a few minutes, she felt a great release come. The inner vow was broken!

Next, we prayed for more holy laughter to come upon

FREE FROM THE PAST

Janet. She laughed and laughed and laughed. From the holy laughter came a release of much rage and healing of the pain-filled childhood years—the root cause of her inner vow being made in the first place. Suddenly, Janet exclaimed, "My face has become unfrozen! My face has become unfrozen! It felt stiff before! I'm a new person!"

She continued to rejoice, saying, "I'm free! I'm free! I'm free!" She had been released from the "prison" in which her inner vow had placed her.

Rose: Still Sucking Her Thumb at Twelve

Negative vows we make in later life also hurt us, but an inner vow is one that is usually established in us in childhood. It is usually forgotten, but it continues to exert a powerful influence over our lives.

Rose was still sucking her thumb at the age of twelve, and she came to us in despair. Her friends made fun of her, and in spite of a great effort on her part, she could not seem to break the habit.

The Lord revealed to us that, at age two, she had made an inner vow not to grow up. With our encouragement, she made the decision that she wanted to grow up and that she would not remain a little girl any longer. With her permission, we then broke that vow in the powerful name of Jesus. We also included a long prayer for the Lord to "grow her up" to her current age of twelve. He did this by His Spirit, a mighty miracle!

When it happened, I knew in the Spirit that she was free. I said, "Rose, suck your thumb."

"No!" she replied. "I don't want to. I've lost all desire to suck my thumb."

During the next several weeks, we saw Rose many times, and she was still free and experiencing an amazing growth in maturity. She had "grown up" to age twelve.

The vow not to grow up is one that a great percentage of us make. Each of us needs to express a willingness to God to grow up and then do spiritual warfare to break the vow that prevents it from happening.

My Inner Vow

When I was about twelve, my parents transferred me from a public school to a private one with much higher scholastic standards. I was warned that it might be difficult for me to attain even passing grades. This was a traumatic experience, and to make matters worse, I was being separated from all of my old friends.

I fiercely determined to do well and overzealously sought to be outstanding in my grades. This offended many of my new peers. To everyone's surprise, including my own, I made the highest grades in my class. This led to jealousy, criticism and rejection from the other students, and that, of course, hurt me deeply.

The whole affair came to the attention of the principal, and one day he called me into his office. He criticized me for my extreme "eagerness" in pursuing excellence. He was probably right, but what he said that day hurt me deeply, and I made an inner vow that I would never again seek excellence.

In spite of many natural talents and much hard studying, I never again made the honor roll—in middle school, high school, college or graduate school. And I could not understand why. That inner vow had become a curse on my life. My ability to be excellent was imprisoned. That vow also negatively affected many other areas of my life, such as business, hobbies, sports and personal relationships.

Some years ago the Lord revealed to me that I had made this damaging inner vow, and since then the Holy Spirit has led me to spend much time breaking it through spiritual warfare, including the deep groanings of self-travail. Over and over I have confessed spiritual truths about being excellent for God, such as *"I am more than a conqueror through Christ Jesus"* and *"I can do all things through Christ who strengtheneth me."* I thank God that Jesus loved me so much that He became a curse for me so that I could be free. The vow has lost its power over me, and I am free to be excellent for the Lord. I, too, have come out of prison.

Rose, Janet, and I were dramatically changed by breaking an inner vow. Is it possible that your life also can be changed by doing the same? Do you need to come out of your self-made prison?

Childhood Inner Vows

As noted in Chapter 1, it is estimated that about twenty-five percent of women are molested sexually in childhood by family members or others, and nearly all of these women make a strong inner vow to shut down their emotions and to distrust all men (and this often includes

God). Because of this, their relationships with other people are doomed to failure, and a happy and fulfilling marriage for them becomes almost impossible.

The deep desire to protect oneself from further hurt causes many to make such inner vows in childhood. An inner vow like Janet's, not to be hurt again, is one of those most frequently made. For many of us, such a vow is powerful and prevents us from becoming vulnerable and transparent in our relationships with others. It keeps "the real me" from being seen or known by others. Such inner vows become the root cause of our having a distrust of men, of women, of preachers or of others. Three of the most damaging inner vows are: "I will never trust anyone again," "I will never show my emotions again," and "In order to be loved, I must earn it."

> *I thank God that Jesus loved me so much that He became a curse for me so that I could be free!*

A Vow to Suppress Our Emotions

When we make a vow to suppress our emotions, it holds us back from childlikeness, from being the person

FREE FROM THE PAST

God has created us to be and from loving and receiving love in the dimension that the Lord has for us. Moreover, it bottles up the rivers of living water, making it difficult to teach, preach, witness or prophesy with the freedom the Lord desires. It also hinders our ability to praise and worship God with the intensity and fullness He merits.

Make a decision, in Jesus' name, to break any destructive inner vows you may have made, and then, in spiritual warfare, shout in tongues for two or three minutes. To break the vow deeply and to open up to the "rivers of living waters" shout in tongues for thirty minutes a day for three days in a row. Many have testified that this changed their lives, and your life will be changed too, as a result of your obedience.

EARNED LOVE VS. UNCONDITIONAL LOVE

God loves us unconditionally, just as we are, and not because of how much we pray, read His Word, fast, give or attend church. We, likewise, should love our children unconditionally. We should love them because they are our children and not because of what they do or become. In most homes, however, love is given on the basis of who has earned it. If you have made an inner vow that you must earn love to be loved, you will find yourself continually striving to be good enough, to be worthy enough, for people to love you—even to be loved by God. And usually you will never feel quite good enough.

Most of us have made this inner vow, or affirmation, that we must earn love, and it is very damaging to our interpersonal relationships. First of all, such a vow causes children to strive for good grades, success in sports, music or in other ways, just to earn love from their parents. Secondly, once they have reached the teenage years, to be accepted by their peers, many start using drugs, having sex and rejecting God. This striving for acceptance is not just a teenage problem; it carries over into later life.

Those who have this problem never feel worthy—unless they are constantly doing things for others. This vow needs to be broken, in the mighty name of Jesus, and our minds need to be renewed to the truth of God's unconditional love. We are made worthy only by the blood of Christ, no other way.

THE CONCLUSION

In conclusion, harmful inner vows cause many problems in our relationships with others and with God. Freedom from them is often the key to major releases. Seek the Lord for a revelation of destructive inner vows in your life, and then break them just as Janet, Rose and I did. This will lead to major, even life-transforming, changes in your life. Breaking these destructive inner vows will help you to be *Free from the Past*.

Chapter 8

Negative Soul Ties, Idolatry and Fragmentation

They are all estranged from me through their idols. ... Repent, and turn yourselves from your idols; and turn away your faces from all your abominations.

Ezekiel 14:5-6

FREE FROM THE PAST

Mental, emotional or physical abuse from key people in our lives causes injurious, often hate-filled, negative soul ties. Such soul ties and the abuse or rejection that causes them also cause a fragmentation, a ripping or tearing of one's heart. It is as though part of our heart is missing. Negative soul ties need to be broken through strong spiritual warfare, and we must be healed from the effects of fragmentation.

ALICE: AN UNHEALTHY ATTRACTION

Alice pleaded with us, "I want to discontinue the relationship, but I feel an unhealthy and unwanted attraction to him. I don't seem to have the will to break away. Please help me to be free!"

For several years, Alice, a lovely black sister, had a male telephone prayer partner. God consistently answered their prayers, and for a year or two, it had been a fulfilling and fruitful relationship. Gradually, however, the man had become more and more controlling. Also, Alice had discovered sexual uncleanness and dishonesty in his life. In the process of their praying together, their souls had become tied together with invisible chains. Now, Alice found herself unable to break free from him, and she was crying to God for help.

The first thing Pattie and I did was ask her if she was willing to forgive her prayer partner for his dishonesty, his uncleanness and his controlling methods. Forgiveness is essential to being set free from such soul ties. She was willing, so we led her through a prayer of forgiveness for the man, including a long prayer of blessing over him, because God commands us to bless our *"enemies."*

We then had Alice pray loudly in tongues. As she was doing this, we laid hands on her for holy laughter. She laughed, laughed and laughed, and soon she broke into deep sobbing for her heartfelt emotional pains. She was undergoing deep self-travail, which is the key to deep and quick inner healing. After a short period of this travail, a deep peace came into her heart.

Now Alice was ready to break the soul tie with her prayer partner. For this, we used an unusual method which the Holy Spirit has given us (and probably others). The secret of it is found in the book of Hebrews:

> *Mental, emotional or physical abuse from key people in our lives causes injurious, often hate-filled, negative soul ties!*

For the word of God is quick, and powerful, and sharper than any two-edged sword, piercing even to the dividing asunder of soul and spirit.

Hebrews 4:12

Somewhat as a prophetic act, we have individuals take *"the sword of the Spirit"* in their hands and powerfully cut the soul tie, usually doing warfare in tongues at the same time. We had Alice do this, and soon the soul tie was completely severed.

Fragmentation of the Heart

Next, in the name of Jesus, we commanded the missing part of Alice's heart, the part given to her male prayer partner, to return. We instructed her to pray: "In Jesus' name, I command the missing part of my heart to come back now."

I said to Alice, "Now take a deep breath (representing the breath of God), and receive back the missing part of your heart."

"I did this," Alice later said, "and soon I felt a great peace. My pains from arthritis evaporated, and the oppressing spirits I had battled for over a year were gone. I feel a great release and peace deep within me," she said. "I feel free." Just that quickly and easily, Alice was set free, and you can be too!

Marilyn: Grief for a Dead Son

"I have never gotten over my son's death of five years ago," said Marilyn. "I am in continual emotional pain over it." Her sadness over her son's death and her unwillingness to let him go had caused a deep and abiding grief in her. Her husband said, "Since our son's death, no one has been able to help Marilyn. She is not able to function as a wife or as a mother. I hope you can help her."

"What my husband's saying is true," continued

Marilyn, "and also I'm still tormented by having been sexually abused by my father and uncle as a little girl." This sexual abuse had caused great shame and emotional pain, which led to a negative, damaging soul tie with her father and uncle. Because of these soul ties established as a child, all the emotional pain that accompanied them and the trauma of the death of her son, Marilyn was emotionally crippled. Through these harmful soul ties, she was emotionally chained to the three of them.

Marilyn expressed her willingness to forgive her father and her uncle, an essential step in being free from harmful soul ties. Pattie and I then asked her to pray a prayer of forgiveness and a special prayer to bless her *"enemies,"* those who had abused her. We then ministered further inner healing to her for this terrible abuse caused by her father and uncle.

After about thirty minutes of inner healing prayer for these wounds, we next broke the negative soul ties with each of them. As these soul-tie chains were broken, a great release took place within Marilyn.

Next, she was ready for the healing of her fragmented, torn heart, caused by the sexual abuse. She was ready to "call back" the missing parts of her heart, given or taken by her father and uncle.

She later reported, "As we did this, I could actually feel and even see many parts of my heart returning, and what a wonderful feeling of wholeness came!"

Marilyn was now ready for the emotional healing and breaking of the negative soul tie with her son. After about fifteen minutes of inner healing prayer for the pain of losing him, with her permission and cooperation, we broke the soul tie with her deceased son, releasing him to Jesus.

When loved ones die, they take with them part of our hearts. Special ministry was needed for Marilyn's fragmented, torn heart to be made whole. She called back into her heart the portion given to her deceased son.

> *When loved ones die, they take with them part of our hearts!*

"How do you feel now, Marilyn?" we enquired.

"Words cannot describe how I feel," she replied. "My husband won't recognize me. I'm a new person. I feel so free, and I have such a deep peace."

The grief was gone, and Marilyn left a new person. Her husband had a new wife, and her children had a new mother.

SHARON: GRIEF FROM HER MOTHER'S DEATH

Our body can be deeply affected by negative emotions, such as bitterness, fear and grief. These harmful emotions can either cause or contribute to arthritis, migraine headaches, cancer, stress and depression.

"Shortly after Mother's death," Sharon told us, "I developed severe chest pains, which continued for five long years. Mother and I had been close, and her death was devastating to me, physically and emotionally. I just can't let my mother go." This resulted in a strong soul tie with her mother that needed to be broken if Sharon was to be free from the resultant grief.

Our Unidentified Grief

Like Sharon, most of us still carry an enormous amount of hidden grief from the death of loved ones. Such grief usually includes a combination of rage, guilt feelings and loneliness from the loss. For example, after twenty years I still had grief over the death of my mother, my father and my grandmother. I still had a soul tie with them that needed to be broken. In recent years, through the *"groanings,"* the self-travail of Romans 8:26, the Lord has set me free from these soul ties, as well as from the grief, and with these releases He has brought a new peace into my life. He will do the same for you.

At our request, Sharon willingly forgave her mother for dying! We have found that most of us have not forgiven our loved ones for leaving us in this way. We resent them leaving us here alone because we need them.

To promote inner healing within her, we then ministered holy laughter to Sharon for the pain of losing her mother. She both laughed and cried until peace came.

As with Alice, we also had Sharon take the sword of the Spirit and cut the soul tie with her deceased mother. We also had her call back the missing, fragmented part of her heart given to her mother. Then, when we asked,

"Sharon, how do you feel?" she replied, "I feel whole on the inside. I feel wonderful."

During this process of inner healing and calling back the fragmented parts of her heart, Sharon received a healing miracle for the severe chest pains. She was totally healed of that condition. We have a great and awesome God, who does all things well.

You, too, can be liberated from existing soul ties with deceased loved ones. You can be free from grief and also healed in your body. God wants your life to be one of wholeness, righteousness, peace and joy.

A Husband and Wife: Both Delivered

A woman was grieving deeply over the death of her father, who had died seven years earlier. I laid hands upon her and ministered to her, and she travailed deeply before the Lord. She was totally set free from the soul tie with her father and from the deep pain of her father's death, and a new joy came into her life.

Her husband, who was sitting beside her, then became aware of the deep sorrow he still had over his own father's death three years earlier. He requested prayer, and he, too, was wonderfully set free of grief. How about you?

James: An Illicit Soul Tie Led to Adultery

James said, "I was the pastor of a thriving church with about three hundred faithful members. My work load was heavy, and I didn't find much time to be with my family or with the Lord. My wife was hard to communicate with and didn't seem to understand me. My highly efficient, lovely church secretary did communicate deeply with me. What a joy it was to express my innermost feelings to her. I was able to share so much with her, things my wife didn't seem to understand."

What was happening to James is known as spiritual adultery, and it usually leads to the forming of a strong negative soul tie between the two individuals. More often than not, it also leads to actual physical adultery.

Like most pastors, James overworked, didn't spend enough time with the Lord or with his family and needed deliverance from a spirit of lust (a problem with most men). A strong soul tie became established with his secretary. She was a lonely person and was drawn to him. Eventually the spiritual adultery mushroomed into an adulterous affair.

James loved his wife, his three lovely children and his church, but when he was advised to break off the affair and get rid of his secretary or he would lose everything, his reply was, "I can't do it. She is life to me." A powerful soul tie, including a spirit of lust, had gripped him so tightly that he didn't see how he could be free of it. It had a grip not only on his emotions, but also on his thinking.

James was deceived. He was sure that this woman, who was not his wife, was life to him, when in fact she was death to him. Sin is like that. It promises life, but brings death. As Paul wrote:

FREE FROM THE PAST

For the wages of sin is death; but the gift of God is eternal life through Jesus Christ our Lord.

Romans 6:23

Because sin had such a strong hold on James, he eventually lost his wife, his children and his church. This same tragedy is being acted out far too often in the lives of pastors, evangelists and other Christian leaders in every part of the world today. Marriages, ministries, careers and sometimes eternal destinies are being destroyed, and no one seems to know what to do about it.

How can these tragedies be prevented? And how can they be healed when they do happen? Understanding the need for deliverance from a spirit of lust and understanding the evil nature of spiritual adultery and the resulting soul ties is a big step.

NEGATIVE SOUL TIES AND IDOLATRY

We are created in need of an intimate relationship with God. When we fail to have a close relationship with Him, we try to fill the void through relationships of various types with people. In doing that, we often develop negative soul ties with some of them.

We also sometimes attempt to fill the void in our lives with things, such as hobbies, sports, alcohol, drugs, sex, pornography, soap operas or even church. This is idolatry, giving to "things" the worship, loyalty or priority which belongs to God alone.

When we develop harmful soul ties with individuals,

we give to them part of our heart or love that should be reserved for God or for others. For example, a strong negative soul tie with a prayer partner can rob our spouse or our children of affection due to them.

We can pick up negative traits and evil spirits from our soul ties. Also we are often controlled by other people through such negative soul ties, or by things (idolatry), and are not free to love and be loved in a healthy, godly way. These soul ties need to be broken.

THE DAMAGE CAUSED BY FRAGMENTATION

We need to focus on breaking the most damaging, strongest soul ties, because these cause a great fragmentation of our hearts. Such soul ties usually come from:

1. Childhood mental, emotional or physical abuse by our parents or by other important authority figures in our lives, or from childhood sexual abuse by our

> *When we fail to have a close relationship with Him, we try to fill the void through relationships of various types with people!*

parents or others (Emotional abuse includes possessive, controlling or smothering love.)
2. Ex-husbands, ex-wives or ex-lovers
3. Anyone in our lives controlling us or our controlling them
4. Any person with whom we had a deep relationship who was involved in the occult (Such occultic soul ties always result in serious fragmentation of the heart.)
5. A spiritual leader, such as a pastor or an evangelist, who has hurt us badly or whom we idolize
6. A church denomination or a cult or even other Christians
7. Aborted children
8. Deceased loved ones, if we are still grieving or have been deeply hurt by them

Childhood Hurts and Negative Soul Ties

In childhood, we develop a strong bonding to our parents. Some of this is good and pleasing to the Lord, but much of it is of a negative nature because of the mistakes they make in raising us. As noted earlier, no matter how good you think your childhood was, most likely you have many forgotten or deeply buried hurts from your past. You may have received very little love or conditional or possessive love. Some of our parents were alcoholics; some had deep emotional or even mental problems. A large number of us have been abused verbally, emotionally and even sexually by one or both of our parents.

Negative Soul Ties, Idolatry and Fragmentation

As we have seen, often we identify being loved with earning love by our accomplishments. We feel we must earn love by doing good things or by being a "good" person.

Our emotional pain leads to unforgiveness, bitterness and enormous amounts of rage toward our parents and, later in life, toward others. This causes us to develop strong negative soul ties with our parents, and through these soul ties, we take on their negative qualities, becoming more and more like them in the process. Although many children of alcoholic parents vow that they will *never* be like their alcoholic parents, the fact is that a great majority of the children of alcoholic parents either become alcoholics or workaholics themselves or marry someone who is.

Those who were abused sexually as children vow that they will protect their own children from being abused in that same way, but the fact is that many of those who were themselves sexually abused as children end up doing the same things to their own children or marrying someone who does.

The good news is that Jesus, on the cross of Calvary, has purchased victory for you and me from all negative soul ties and their harmful effects. It comes through forgiveness, inner healing and deliverance.

These childhood hurts also blind us to truth. We see our parents' negative qualities in God, in our spouse and in others. This, in turn, causes us to distrust God and everyone else.

Your deep forgiveness of your parents and breaking

the negative soul ties with them sets you free to establish healthy relationships with others. If you are married, it enables you to *"leave"* your parents and to *"cleave"* to your spouse—to be one in spirit, soul and body with him or her.

A GODLY SOUL TIE WITH OUR MARRIAGE PARTNER

As we noted in an earlier chapter, Jesus said:

A man shall leave father and mother, and shall cleave to his wife: and they twain shall be one flesh. Wherefore they are no more twain, but one flesh. Matthew 19:5-6

What does "leaving" your parents mean? It primarily means being set free from over-dependence on them—emotionally, financially or spiritually. This involves breaking negative soul ties with them. "Leaving" applies to both husband and wife, and this separation, this breaking of negative soul ties, in-

> *"Leaving" applies to both husband and wife, and this separation, this breaking of negative soul ties, includes ex-spouses, ex-lovers and even some of your close friends!*

cludes ex-spouses, ex-lovers and even some of your close friends.

This doesn't mean that you should give up good friends or that you are being disloyal to your parents. When God sets you free from negative soul ties and heals you of fragmentation, you will have a more healthy relationship with your parents, your friends and your spouse.

Your first loyalty should now be to your wife or husband. There must be no running back and forth to Mother or Dad—either in person, by telephone or emotionally. The negative soul tie, the negative emotional bonding with your parents, must be completely broken. You must *"leave"* them so that you can *"cleave"* to your spouse. This is the only way you can become truly one flesh with your spouse—united in spirit, soul and body. You will now be joined to your marriage partner with a greatly beneficial, godly soul tie.

Correct Priorities

Marriage demands correct priorities and one of them is that you must never put your children before your spouse. This includes children from a previous marriage (although you must love them and protect them from an abusive marriage partner). God must be first in your life, your marriage partner second, your children third, your job fourth and your ministry fifth. If your priorities are right, you will have a dynamic, successful ministry,

FREE FROM THE PAST

whether as an interceding housewife, a witnessing plumber or a big-name evangelist.

SOUL TIES: NEW CONVERTS AND HUNGRY CHRISTIANS

For those of you who are new Christians (or for older Christians who desire to be greatly used by God), God wants you to break those soul ties with your former drinking, gambling or even fishing buddies. Unless these individuals become truly converted and sold-out to Jesus, they will be a bad influence on you. Your old habits still have power to pull you back into the "prison" of sin. You should not even enjoy being with those worldly companions. You are a new person in Christ.

You need to become a member of a dynamic Christian church where the Word of God is preached and the power of God is present. You need to find new friends who love Jesus and think and act like you do.

It may even be hard to spend time with certain family members who live, talk and think differently from the "new you." Their company will pull you down. Paul wrote:

> *Wherefore come out from among them, and be ye separate, saith the Lord, and touch not the unclean thing ... and ye shall be my sons and daughters, saith the Lord Almighty.* 2 Corinthians 6:17-18

God is calling all of us to walk in intimacy with Him. What a blessing! What a privilege!

THE CONCLUSION

Jesus came into the world to accomplish restoration in those who would receive Him. His work was (and still is):

To heal the brokenhearted, to preach deliverance to the captives, and recovering of sight to the blind, to set at liberty them that are bruised.   Luke 4:18

We all have many unhealed hurts, unrevealed sin, negative soul ties and fragmented hearts. The good news is that you can be set free just as Alice, Marilyn and countless others have been. Using just a few of the simple Holy Spirit methods, or tools, discussed in this chapter will bring tremendous releases into your life and, through you, into the lives of others. You, too, can be *Free from the Past.*

CHAPTER 9

THE RENEWED MIND AND INNER HEALING

And be not conformed to this world: but be ye transformed by the renewing of your mind, that ye may prove what is that good, and acceptable, and perfect, will of God.   Romans 12:2

> *For to be carnally minded is death; but to be spiritually minded is life and peace.* Romans 8:6

THE RENEWAL OF JOSHUA'S AND DAVID'S MINDS

The Lord ordered Joshua to meditate on His word *"day and night"* so that his mind would be renewed to God's way of thinking and he would become courageous enough to accomplish the mighty tasks that lay ahead of him:

> *This book of the law shall not depart out of thy mouth; but thou shalt meditate therein day and night, that thou mayest observe to do according to all that is written therein: for then thou shalt make thy way prosperous, and then thou shalt have good success.*
> Joshua 1:8

David experienced this same renewal. He wrote:

> *Blessed is the man that walketh not in the counsel of the ungodly, nor standeth in the way of sinners, nor*

The Lord ordered Joshua to meditate on His word "day and night" so that his mind would be renewed to God's way of thinking!

sitteth in the seat of the scornful. But his delight is in the law of the LORD; *and in his law doth he meditate day and night. And he shall be like a tree planted by the rivers of water, that bringeth forth his fruit in his season; his leaf also shall not wither; and whatsoever he doeth shall prosper.* Psalm 1:1-3

It was through *"day and night"* meditation on the Word of God that David came to be so close to God's heart.

KENNETH COPELAND'S RENEWED MIND

A few years after his salvation, Kenneth and Gloria Copeland were in debt, often sick and with little understanding of their calling. At the leading of the Holy Spirit, he obtained all of Kenneth Hagin, Sr.'s tapes and listened to them day and night for about a month. The result was that it changed his whole way of thinking to God's way. He then continued throughout the years filling his heart daily with the Word of God.

Jerry Savelle, Kenneth Copeland's spiritual son, followed in his footsteps and listened to his tapes for a few months *"day and night"* and it turned his life around. Both of these men have large ministries, extending all over the world. More importantly, they show forth the love of God in loving, happy marriages, and in Spirit-filled children who love them and even work with them.

I have listened to twenty-four tapes of Kenneth Copeland and thirty tapes of Jerry Savelle some seven times each, and I have listened to some forty of Thurman Scrivner's tapes on faith about ten times each. I, too,

Death and Life in Our Words

It is correct to say, "I must not do that," when we know that something is not God's will for us. There are many things in the Christian life that may seem difficult, but God will give us the strength and anointing to do them.

When we say "I can't," however, we are siding with the devil against the Word of God, and we will not be able to accomplish the things God desires in our life! When you repeatedly state, *"I can do all things through Christ which strengtheneth me"* (Philippians 4:13), then you can do them because the wisdom and power of God will be with you. There is tremendous power in the way we think and the words that we choose to express our thoughts.

We cannot have a negative mind and a victorious life. A life with ungodly beliefs and a life of victory cannot go together. We must renew our minds to God's Word, to His principles and laws and then speak them:

> *Death and life are in the power of the tongue: and they that love it shall eat the fruit thereof.* Proverbs 18:21

Casting Down All Negative Thoughts

We must cast down all negative thoughts that the

devil brings to our minds and replace them with faith thoughts. In this way, we fight the good fight of faith. There is tremendous victory in having our minds in agreement with God's Word. This is what faith is: believing and taking action on God's Word, on His promises.

We need not be victims of the past, nor of people, nor of present circumstances. The Lord is our Shepherd. Trust Him and His promises. He will never leave you nor forsake you. Let Him be in control of your life.

We must renew our minds to the truths that we can, indeed, do all things through our mighty Lord Jesus, and that in every difficulty, God will be the Source of supplying all our needs. The Scriptures promise:

> *We are more than conquerors through him that loved us.* Romans 8:37

> *But my God shall supply all your need according to his riches in glory by Christ Jesus.* Philippians 4:19

Appropriating these truths will mightily change your life. When you believe that through Jesus Christ you can be successful in every area of your life, God will bring it to pass (see Psalm 37:5). When you disbelieve or doubt, you attract "reasons" and negative people to support your disbelief. Doubt, disbelief and a subconscious will to fail (the not-really-wanting-to-succeed mentality) is responsible for most failures. This is a demonic stronghold that needs to be broken through the renewal of your mind.

FREE FROM THE PAST

MOVING FROM DARKNESS TO LIGHT

What does it mean, then, to have your mind renewed, and what will it accomplish for you? It is a complete change in the way you view life and relationships. It is moving from darkness into light, from the natural or carnal way of thinking to the spiritual. To have a renewed mind means to have the way you think changed by the Holy Spirit to the way God thinks and believes. You begin to see things from God's perspective, from His viewpoint. He has said:

> *My thoughts are not your thoughts, neither are your ways my ways, saith the LORD. For as the heavens are higher than the earth, so are my ways higher than your ways, and my thoughts than your thoughts.*
>
> Isaiah 55:8-9

In this way, faith in God—in His truth, in His principles—will become a way of life for you, and you will experience and live in the peace that passes all understanding.

The way you think will affect your words and your actions and, therefore, will determine whether you live in victory or defeat, in fulfillment or frustration. Jesus said:

> *A good man out of the good treasure of the heart bringeth forth good things: and an evil man out of the evil treasure bringeth forth evil things.*
>
> Matthew 12:35

The Renewed Mind and Inner Healing

As your mind becomes renewed to God's truths, by having the Word of God planted deeply in your heart, you will bring forth good things in your life—good words and good actions—which, in turn, will cause you to be more than a conqueror through Christ Jesus.

Revisiting the Law of Sowing and Reaping

If you insulate a house well, you will save money and be more comfortable. If you eat nutritiously and exercise correctly, you will have a strong body, more energy and less sickness. If you pay your tithes, God will bless you financially. If you delight yourself in the Lord, He will give you the desires of your heart (see Psalm 37:4). You "sow" an action, and you "reap" a result.

> *All of life is based on cause and effect, sowing and reaping!*

All of life is based on cause and effect, sowing and reaping. The Bible says:

> *Be not deceived; God is not mocked: for whatsoever a man soweth, that shall he also reap. For he that soweth to his flesh shall of the flesh reap corruption; but he that soweth to the Spirit shall of the Spirit reap life everlasting.* Galatians 6:7-8

FREE FROM THE PAST

Learn to sow what is pleasing to God, and you will reap untold benefits.

GOD'S SUCCESS PRINCIPLES

God does not promise you a life without trials, but He has promised you victory in every trial:

> *There hath no temptation taken you but such as is common to man: but God is faithful, who will not suffer you to be tempted above that ye are able; but will with the temptation also make a way to escape, that ye may be able to bear it.* 1 Corinthians 10:13

> *If we suffer, we shall also reign with him: if we deny him, he also will deny us.* 2 Timothy 2:12

God has success principles that apply to every area of your life. His truth, His Word, His principles and His laws will set you free from every bondage, every stronghold, and will produce prosperity in every area of your life.

The Lord instructed Joshua to renew his mind through the Word of God. As we have seen, the Lord spoke to him:

> *This book of the law shall not depart out of thy mouth; but thou shalt meditate therein day and night, that thou mayest observe to do according to all that is writ-*

ten therein: for then thou shalt make thy way prosperous, and then thou shalt have good success.

Joshua 1:8

Renewing your mind to God's Word, to His success principles, will cause you to "sow" actions that will "reap" success in every area of your life, including your relationships with God, your family and your friends, as well as success in your job and in your finances.

Your Mind Becomes Conformed to What You Meditate On

You must be careful not to behold or focus on the wrong images, including the wrong image of yourself! You need to be full of the Word, God's truth, His promises, so you won't be overwhelmed by the problems of life. Focus on the promises of God, not the problems, not the mountains in your life.

When necessary, the Holy Spirit will anoint you to glance, not in fear, but in faith, at the problems of life. But you must look at your problems, your trials, as challenges, as opportunities for God to show His greatness. He has many miracles waiting for you. Reach out by faith and grab them!

Through the mighty power of the Holy Spirit or, negatively, through the power of the enemy, you are transformed into what you meditate on—good or bad, godly or ungodly. Meditating, pondering and reflecting on the Word of God will teach you His principles, His

FREE FROM THE PAST

> *If you meditate on the problems in your life instead of on the promises of God's abundant supply, you will become carnal and fearful in your thinking!*

laws, and this will renew your mind. These principles and laws become birthed within you. They will become part of you. Meditation on His Word will cause you to become more and more like Him!

The Word of God states:

But we all, with unveiled face, beholding as in a mirror the glory of the Lord, are being transformed into the same image from glory to glory, just as by the Spirit of the Lord. 2 Corinthians 3:18, NKJ

If you meditate on the faults of others, you will become like them. If you meditate on the pleasures of the world, you will become like people of the world. If you meditate on the problems in your life instead of on the promises of God's abundant supply, you will become carnal and fearful in your thinking, and this will block God's miracle-working power in your life.

Praise is a language of faith. Complaining is an attitude, or mind-set, of unbelief and even rebellion. It includes self-pity and even blaming God! The Lord desires us to praise Him continually for the blessings of life and also for the trials in our lives and also that we be set free from complaining and unbelief! David said:

> *I will bless the LORD AT ALL TIMES: his praise shall CONTINUALLY be in my mouth.*
> Psalm 34:1 (Emphasis Added)

Some people are willing to praise God *in* their trials, but they can't understand why we should praise God *for* those trials. "Aren't trials caused, directly or indirectly, by the devil?" they might ask. This is true, but God is in control of our lives, and He desires to bring good out of every bad situation. Praising Him for the trials and hardships of life is a language of faith. It shows we trust God, and it releases Him to work on our behalf, to bring good out of the situation.

Praising for the trial removes fear and enhances our relationship with God. Again, His Word tells us:

> *And we know that all things work together for good to them that love God, to them who are the called according to his purpose.*
> Romans 8:28

> *Giving thanks always FOR all things unto God and the Father in the name of our Lord Jesus Christ.*
> Ephesians 5:20

> *My brethren, count it all joy when ye fall into divers temptations.*
> James 1:2

FREE FROM THE PAST

Joseph came to know that God brings good out of evil. Years after his brothers sold him into slavery in Egypt, he said to them:

Ye thought evil against me; but God meant it unto good.
Genesis 50:20

Over the years, Pattie and I have experienced great blessings from praising God for trials in our lives. For example, our car broke down when we were on our way to a revival meeting in Pittsburgh. Right there on the side of the highway (much to the chagrin of our embarrassed daughter, who hid in the back seat), the two of us danced and praised God *for* the breakdown. Yes, right there on the side of the road, in public.

And what happened? Within three minutes, an empty car carrier stopped. The driver pulled our car on top and allowed the four of us to squeeze into the cab with him. Then he sped off, taking us to where we could get help, and we arrived on time in Pittsburgh to preach that night. God does all things well.

Once, when Pattie was driving in Virginia, a drunk driver hit our car and then left the scene of the accident. Pattie praised God in the dance on the highway, and when I heard of the accident, I also praised God *for* the trial. In the end, the driver returned to the scene of the accident and paid for our damages.

Last year I was closing a roll-up metal self-storage door and caught three of my fingers in it. When I finally got my fingers out of the door, I was in such terrible pain that I feared permanent damage. With Pattie's encouragement, I praised God *for* the accident and the pain. To my amazement, the pain soon vanished, and there was not even a bruise on my fingers, although the metal of the accordion-like door was bent in three places where my fingers had been caught!

Trust God and know that He will never let any trial come to you unless He can bring good out of it. Praise Him even for the small irritations of life. He will often teach you valuable lessons through them. Murmuring, complaining and self-pity will leave, and a new peace and faith will come into your life.

I encourage you to read Merlin Carothers' book, *Power in Praise* (BridgeLogos, Alachua, Florida: 1972), on the awesome victories and power you can receive from praising God for the trials of life.

Adamic Sin and Ungodly Beliefs

Because of Adamic sin and the generational sins of our family line, we live in a world of sin, fear, deception, lies and half-truths. From birth, because of hurts (including negative words and ideas) and rejection by loved ones, our minds have been programmed to a multitude of ungodly beliefs. These wrong beliefs—incorrect, ungodly ways of thinking—become demonic strongholds in a person's life. They don't just make life more difficult; they actually squeeze us like an octopus. They become strongholds that trap us in a spiritual prison of wrong thinking.

FREE FROM THE PAST

Each one of us, to a large extent, lives his life with these wrong beliefs. We believe lies about ourselves, about God and about others. It is difficult for us to trust God in our hearts when every important person in our lives has let us down, deeply hurt us or disappointed us.

Most people are afraid of and rebel against surrendering their beliefs, ideas and self-control to anyone. This includes God, because they assign to Him the ungodly qualities of their parents and other authority figures. Such wrong beliefs are strongholds and must be broken. Our minds must be renewed to God's way of thinking.

GETTING RID OF UNGODLY BELIEFS

Your mind cannot be renewed to God's way of thinking until you are willing to be changed, and until you know how to give up your present ungodly beliefs—your ways of controlling your own life. God wants you totally dependent upon Him.

As emphasized throughout this book, one of the major purposes of inner healing and deliverance is to change us on the inside, to produce within us the character of Christ. This includes the mind of Christ—the way He thinks. Therefore, having our minds renewed to God's way of thinking, to His principles and laws, is the most important spiritual tool or principle of inner healing.

The first stage in the renewal of your mind is getting rid of your old ungodly beliefs and ways of thinking, including fears, distrust and rebellion against man and God—even against change itself. This will prepare you for the next stage in the renewal of your mind, a change to a whole new way of thinking—God's way of thinking, reflecting His truths, His Word, His wisdom, His love. When this happens, yours will be a life surrendered to God, a life of peace and joy:

> For the kingdom of God is not meat and drink; but righteousness, and peace, and joy in the Holy Ghost.
>
> Romans 14:17

It will be a life of greatly enriched relationships with friends, with loved ones and with God through the Lord Jesus Christ. I'm sure you want this.

> *Most people are afraid of and rebel against surrendering their beliefs, ideas and self-control to anyone!*

RENEWAL OF THE MIND FOR PHYSICAL HEALING

With a stressful look on her face, Alicia, a lovely black sister, approached Pattie and me and confided, "I've had migraine headaches for more than ten years, and they never leave completely. My head is always in pain and pressure. It makes it hard to be a good mother or wife. Can you help me?"

Thank God, we were able to say that we could help

her. We ministered extensively to her for the healing of deep, rage-filled wounds from the past—the root cause of the migraines. Then, in the name of Jesus, we commanded the spirit of migraine to leave permanently. For the first time in years, she was pain-free, healed by the mighty power of God. Isn't our God wonderful?

We then instructed Alicia in the importance of thanking the Lord repeatedly for His mighty healing miracle in her life. We also had her to repeatedly quote healing scriptures. This is essential to receiving and keeping your miracle. It enables you to believe in your heart that you are healed. Your mind becomes renewed to this truth.

KEEPING YOUR HEALING

In the physical healing ministry, one of the greatest lacks in the Body of Christ is the failure to teach Christians how to keep their healing. If you follow certain spiritual principles, you will rarely lose your healing.

When persons are healed and the pains or other symptoms leave, in most cases the devil will bring the symptoms back—to convince them that they are not healed. Your mind needs to be renewed to the important spiritual truth that the return of pains or other symptoms does not mean you have lost your healing. This is a trial of your faith, and you must contend fervently for your healing. As the Scriptures declare:

For we walk by faith, not by sight.
                                            2 Corinthians 5:7, NKJ

The Renewed Mind and Inner Healing

We walk by faith in God's promises, not by what we see or feel. Walking by faith and not by sight is one of the most important principles of faith, and our minds need to be deeply renewed to this principle.

Furthermore, when you are believing for a great miracle in your life, whether for healing, finances, family relationships, open doors of ministry, revival in your church or some other type of miracle, circumstances usually get worse before the miracle comes. You must stand on God's promises and on His faithfulness. Never focus on your circumstances, nor on what you reason with your natural mind. The miracle will come. The Bible tells us:

> *And let us not be weary in well doing: for in due season we shall reap, if we faint not.*   Galatians 6:9

With ten years of nonstop migraines, it would be extremely difficult for Alicia to believe in her heart that she was healed—particularly when she felt the pains returning. Her mind needed to be renewed to the awesome truth that she was, indeed, healed. She needed to be taught how to take authority over any returning migraine pain sent by the devil and to stand, by faith, on the promise that she was healed. Here are some written instructions we gave to Alicia so that her mind would be renewed to the truth necessary to keep her healing. Use them to keep your healing too, or even to receive it:

1. **During the next twenty-four hours, thank God at least twenty-five times for healing you!**

FREE FROM THE PAST

Declare to our Lord, "Jesus, I am healed through Your shed blood. I am healed, I am healed! And I thank You, I thank You, I thank You for my healing. Thank You, Jesus." Again, do it twenty-five times.

> *Get angry at Satan if he tries to put any pain back on you!*

2. Command, in the name of Jesus, any returning pains (or other symptoms) to go, to go, to go.

Get angry at Satan if he tries to put any pain back on you. Jesus took your sickness on the cross. He loves you! You are healed! If even a small amount of pain returns, command it to go. In this way, fight *"the good fight of faith."*

3. Testify to at least three or four people about your healing.

Tell them exactly, in detail, the miracle God has given you. Brag about Jesus!

And they overcame him by the blood of the Lamb, and by the word of their testimony. Revelation 12:11

When you have done these three things, if you still have any pain or other symptoms or if you have a serious

The Renewed Mind and Inner Healing

or long-standing condition such as Alicia had, read out loud the following scriptures three or more times each day (fifty times a day would be much better), and do it for one week:

Who his own self bare our sins in his own body on the tree, that we, being dead to sins, should live unto righteousness: by whose stripes ye were healed.
1 Peter 2:24

Personalize it and repeat many times, "By whose stripes, I was and am healed."

Who forgiveth all thine iniquities; who healeth all thy diseases.   Psalm 103:3

Personalize it. Say *"Who healeth all MY diseases."*
Keep praising Jesus for your healing. He is wonderful. He is mighty. He is our Savior, our Healer and our Deliverer. He has healed you.

You have received the healing Jesus purchased for you on the cross at Calvary through His shed blood. He doesn't want you to lose it. The devil will try to steal it from you by bringing back pains or other symptoms to make you think you have lost your healing. Insist on your healing, and it will be yours permanently.

Please feel free to copy the above instructions for "Keeping Your Healing" and make them available to others.

FREE FROM THE PAST

The Conclusion

We have described in this book various inner healing methods the Holy Spirit uses to remove from our lives much of the roots of negativity, unbelief, lust, rage, fears and other ungodly ways of thinking. This paves the way for *"day and night"* meditation on the Word of God to renew our minds deeply to God's victorious ways of thinking and living.

As you become a doer of the Word and live out these truths in everyday life, they will further transform your thinking, health, actions and life. You will have a new and deeper love for God and greatly enhanced relationships with the people around you. You will be *Free from the Past* to live victoriously in every area of your life and to excitedly look forward to the future.

CHAPTER 10

EASY STEPS TO LIFE-TRANSFORMING INNER HEALING (AND DELIVERANCE)

The previous chapters covered many principles for receiving and ministering inner healing and deliverance. I hope you have found these principles to be exciting, informative and easy to put into practice. Even a little understanding of them will aid you incredibly in being set free and in setting others free as well. I strongly recommend that you review these previous chapters a number of times until the simple principles contained in them become a part of you. Your life will never be the same. Now, in this chapter, I want to summarize these simple principles into steps for inner healing.

There are many layers of hurts in all of our lives, and it would normally take years for them to be removed. But don't be discouraged. You have reason to be excited. Inner healing can come quickly. This process can be sped up greatly! Even one or two weeks of fifteen to thirty minutes daily of deep self-travail or holy laughter can have life-changing results for you. I will show you how easily this can be done:

Step 1. Make a list of the major hurts and disappointments throughout your life, focusing on your childhood years.

Rejection, emotional hurts and abuse from your mother, dad and other family members are the most important. I had twenty-one names on my list. List all the people, including religious leaders, who have hurt or disappointed you greatly and the resultant hurts and disappointments.

Again, all of us live in much denial, even of the fact that we are in denial. We run from painful truths. We need to face the truth of how greatly our lives have been affected by hurts of the past and cooperate with the Holy

Spirit in permitting Him to set us free. Steps two through eight will show you how to be healed from these various hurts on your list.

Now decide to be a forgiving person. Review that list you have just made, and begin to pray for big blessings upon the lives of those who hurt you, and do it with forgiveness. This frees you from the past. Jesus has instructed us to bless those who curse us and to love our enemies (see Matthew 5:44). The Lord also has commanded us to judge not and condemn not, and to forgive. We must not judge others but bless them in prayer, and sometimes in other ways as well.

> *Rejection, emotional hurts and abuse from your mother, dad and other family members are the most important!*

Step 2. Begin shouting very loudly in tongues in the privacy of your home, or in your automobile.

At home, you can do this either standing up or lying on your face on the floor. I often shout in tongues and travail while driving in my automobile. Even a few minutes of this shouting will help release your suppressed emotions. Shouting in tongues will often cause a cleansing and/or inner healing to take place.

If you do not speak in tongues, see Chapter 2 and the appendix on the baptism in the Holy Spirit and how to receive it. This is a free gift from God, and you don't have to earn it or deserve it. You do have to hunger for it and desire more of God in your life in order to receive it. But God has it for you now!

Step 3. Continue shouting in tongues for about two or three minutes until self-travail comes, the "*groanings*" of Romans 8:26!

Shouting in tongues will help you to open up to the Holy Spirit so that self-travail—sobbing, groaning, crying or even anointed screaming (scream into a pillow or in the car)—can more easily begin for the hurts in your life. But you must, in childlike faith, cooperate with the Holy Spirit. He will not force His blessings upon you. As we have seen, such self-travail is the key to rapid, dramatic, life-changing inner healing.

Focus on a deep hurt in your life, rejection or a great disappointment, such as your marriage, your work, your church or your childhood. Then cooperate with the Holy Spirit in opening up to self-travail for the healing of your hurt or disappointment.

How do we cooperate with the Lord? You may be thinking, "I don't want it to be in the flesh. If God wants me to scream or to laugh, He will cause it to happen." The primary cause of Christians being "in the flesh" is our fear of being in the flesh, the fear that we will not be in the Spirit. Because of such fear, we fail to open up to the Holy Spirit as He tries to bring upon us holy laughter, travail, groanings or even holy screaming. We hold back from prophesying, giving a message in tongues or delivering a word of knowledge to a friend, pastor or other leader. Fear binds us from cooperating with the Holy Spirit.

So be childlike, be bold and be obedient to the promptings of the Holy Spirit. If you feel sobbing coming, you must yield and start sobbing. If you feel holy laughter coming, then you must start laughing. If you feel a scream could begin, you must yield to it. How? By faith, just start screaming!

Don't worry about being in the flesh. In faith, you are cooperating with the Holy Spirit. It will be "in the Spirit!" It will be "anointed!" It will be *"bread"* and not *"a stone!"* You will be blessed awesomely.

If you are at home, keep a pillow handy to cover up your loud travail. I travail almost every day in the automobile, so I don't disturb anyone. Try it. It is an excellent place to travail before the Lord. Jesus said:

> *Verily I say unto you, Except ye be converted, and become as little children, ye shall not enter into the kingdom of heaven.* Matthew 18:3

As we noted previously, the Word also states:

> *But God hath chosen the foolish things of the world to confound the wise.* 1 Corinthians 1:27

FREE FROM THE PAST

So be childlike. Show your hunger for more of God. By faith, in childlike simplicity, just do it. Laugh, travail and even scream. God is going to set you free.

The longer you speak in tongues, the more life-transforming your inner healing will be. You may need to repeat this step of moving into self-travail many times in one particular session of prayer.

> *Holy laughter for specific hurts will produce deep inner healing!*

Step 4. If self-travail does not come quickly, then ask the Lord for holy laughter for your hurts.

Holy laughter for specific hurts will produce deep inner healing. It will also help you to open up to self-travail. The greater the emotional pain, the more important it is to laugh in the Spirit about it. If your hurt is truly "no laughing matter," then you must laugh long and hard at it.

To help holy laughter flow, you must cooperate with the Holy Spirit. There are several things you can do:

1. Pray very loudly in tongues (shouting is best).

2. By faith, "prime the pump" with "Hee, hee! Ha, ha! Ho, ho!" about specific hurts in your life. If laughter still hasn't come, then try, "Ho, ho! Ha, ha!

Hee, hee!" This sounds totally foolish, but as indicated earlier, the Bible does say: *"But God hath chosen the foolish things of the world to confound the wise"* (1 Corinthians 1:27).

These "laughter" words (Ho, ho! Ha, ha! Hee, hee!) are heavily anointed by the Lord and are holy words. They will either lead us into deep holy laughter or into self-travail or both. (See Chapter 4, "Inner Healing through Holy Laughter.")

Again, God wants hunger and childlike humility from us. Cooperate with the Lord. In faith, in expectancy and with your eyes closed, try out a few Hee, hee's, Ha, ha's and Ho, ho's for a deep hurt in your life. You may be amazed at what happens!

3. Force yourself to laugh loudly. Be determined that you are going to be set free.

Next, move on to Step 5.

Step 5. In Jesus' name, through spiritual warfare, break the power of generational curses (generational iniquity) unto the third and fourth generation in your family line.

We need to "pray through" until we know we have the victory in every generational area that involves a curse—a negative generational inheritance. With great authority, in the mighty name of Jesus, do spiritual warfare until you feel a witness of the Spirit that the curse is broken. Warfare in English is effective and best, at times, but I have found that warfare in tongues can be even more powerful. Try it, and do it often.

It may take a number of sessions of heavy spiritual warfare to obtain significant victories over generational curses in your family history. For example, as noted earlier, I had to break the generational curse of occultism in my life in several different areas of involvement. These included the ouija board, the pendulum, visiting a fortune-teller and trying to hypnotize someone. I spent a number of days in much spiritual warfare, including self-travail, to break these curses. Effective prayer is hard work! (See Chapter 6, "Breaking the Power of Generational Iniquity.")

Step 6. Follow steps two through five above at least two or three times a week for several weeks!

This is of great importance. There are many layers of hurts and many new areas that the Holy Spirit wants to heal. You will need much more inner healing and deliverance.

Step 7. Feed much on the Word of God, the Bible, renewing your mind from being partially negative to being positive.

The Bible tells us that we must meditate on the Word of God *"day and night"*—not just occasionally. Read good books and listen to good CDs on faith. Each day, force yourself, discipline yourself, to speak only words of faith, for we walk *"by faith, not by sight."*

Speak to Jesus from your heart (not just mentally) seven times a day for one week the following scriptures. As you do, be aware that He is present with you. Tell Him how much you love Him:

Nay, in all these things we are more than conquerors through him that loved us. Romans 8:37

I can do all things through Christ which strengtheneth me. Philippians 4:13

But my God shall supply all your need according to his riches in glory by Christ Jesus. Philippians 4:19

OTHER SPECIAL STEPS TO FOLLOW TO WALK IN VICTORY

Here are a few other steps that will ensure victory in your life:

1. Develop a life of praise and worship.

Begin with at least fifteen minutes a day alone with God, just praising and worshipping Him. Sing songs of worship to the Lord Jesus Christ. Much of your praise and worship, however, should be in tongues. Then increase this time to twenty minutes, and then more as you feel the desire.

FREE FROM THE PAST

Make a list of the many blessings in your life—everything good, including His shed blood, your salvation, the baptism in the Holy Spirit, His friendship, your loved ones, your home, your health and your country. Praise Him often for all of these many blessings in your life.

2. Develop a spirit of thanksgiving in place of complaining.

Whenever self-pity tries to rise up, begin praising God for the many blessings in your life. Complaining and self-pity are faith killers. Thanksgiving is a language of faith and appreciation.

3. All of us need to repent for sins of unforgiveness or grumbling and complaining about hurts and other disappointments in our lives. Be sure we have forgiven God and ourselves!

This includes the judging of others and the desire for revenge. Ask the Lord to search your heart, particularly about judging and criticizing your mother and father and, secondly, your marriage partner.

4. Never condemn yourself. God loves you, and you must also. Confess God's promises over your life.

Godly conviction is good, and it brings victorious repentance. Condemnation of oneself brings self-pity, unbelief and spiritual death. Avoid it.

THE CONCLUSION

Jesus loves us so greatly. He has taken our pain, our sickness, our fears, our hurts, our rejections, our shame and even our disappointments upon Himself:

> *Surely he hath borne our griefs, and carried our sorrows.*
> Isaiah 53:4

Through His shed blood on the cross of Calvary, Jesus has purchased total victory for us in every area of our lives! He has given us the principles to follow to walk in complete victory in life. Inner healing is a free love gift from Him, purchased with His blood. Choose to be free, and don't reject His gift.

Follow even a few of the simple God-given principles in this book, and you will be set free to walk in greatly increased joy and intimacy with God and others. You can be released from the hurts, pains and disappointments of life and become an instrument for setting others free. You can become the person God created you to be. Jesus wants to free you to be able to give and receive love and to

> **Whenever self-pity tries to rise up, begin praising God for the many blessings in your life!**

FREE FROM THE PAST

enjoy greatly improved relationships with family members, friends, co-workers and with God. You, too, can be *Free from the Past*.

APPENDIX

How To Receive the Baptism in the Holy Spirit and the Gift of Speaking in Other Tongues

* To be deeply refilled with the Holy Spirit, begin at step number 5.

FREE FROM THE PAST

SURRENDER TO HIM

If you are not a born-again Christian, first invite Jesus into your heart. Surrender your life to Him. This is a lifetime commitment.

If you have been born-again but are living in sin, you must repent before seeking the Holy Spirit. This means deciding to change, turning your back on sin and seeking God diligently. Repent for the sins of unforgiveness, unbelief, grumbling, complaining, criticizing others, dishonoring your parents or marriage partner, dishonesty and impure sexual thoughts, words or actions.

HUNGER FOR IT

Next, we need to be childlike and greatly desire this priceless free gift from God and to hunger for more of Him in our lives. The Baptism of the Holy Spirit is a free gift from the Almighty Himself! No one is worthy of it, and no one can earn it by good works. You receive this experience to be able to fulfill your destiny, particularly to be conformed to the image of Christ and to walk in greater intimacy with the Father through Jesus.

The baptism in the Holy Spirit will immediately give you a greater anointing to minister to others, whether it is in preaching, teaching, singing, witnessing, praying for the sick or delivering the oppressed. It will also bring a new dimension of joy and peace into your life.

The gift of tongues that accompanies the baptism in the Spirit will enhance your prayer life tremendously. So the sooner you can receive it, the better. Also get your children filled with the Spirit at a young age, even as early as age four.

As noted earlier in the book, new converts and millions of Christians in every denomination and in every nation are receiving the baptism in the Holy Spirit and speaking in other tongues. Fifteen years ago it was already estimated that there were at least 240 million Spirit-filled believers worldwide. Many seek this experience because it brings more power, joy and a greater love for Jesus into the lives of all those who receive it.

THE RECEIVING

You receive the baptism in the Spirit by faith—in the following way (It is not absolutely necessary, but it can be quite helpful to have a Spirit-filled Christian lay hands on you while you receive):

(1) Raise your head very high, and also lift your hands. With your eyes closed, picture Jesus in front of you. This helps you to open your spirit and to surrender more fully to God. This may be difficult and seem unnatural at first because it makes you feel defenseless. Do it by faith.

(2) Praise God loudly (shouting is best) and rapidly, saying, "I love You, Jesus." Do this for just a minute or two, but loudly and rapidly. God lives in the midst of the praises of His people.

(3) After a minute or two of shouting "I love You, Jesus," stop English totally and suddenly. Then immediately start speaking words or syllables you don't understand (even if you think you are making them up). Those strange sounds or words will be from God. You can do it. Remember, don't speak one more word of English. You must open your mouth and speak words you don't understand. As you do this, you are beginning to speak in tongues. God will give you what you are asking for—the gift of tongues. You may think you are making it up, but those words are from God. They are *"bread and not a stone, fish and not a serpent"* (Luke 11:11-13). Continue to speak those God-given unknown words, and the Lord will give you more. Your experience will become deeper and deeper.

(4) It would be greatly desirable to continue speaking in tongues on your first day of being baptized in the Holy Spirit for thirty minutes to two hours. Speak in tongues off and on all day during this first day. It will deepen your experience greatly. Then speak or sing in tongues every day. What you have received is a language of glory, and you will become more aware of God's presence as you use it. You will get your prayers answered more quickly, and the Bible will become alive to you in a new dimension.

Appendix

(5) Step out in faith and speak or sing in a second language and then a third. You can speak or sing in *"divers [many] kinds of tongues"*—not just one (1 Corinthians 12:10). Praying in many new tongues will immensely deepen your experience.

(6) Be sure to speak and sing in tongues every day, preferably at least thirty minutes a day. Your tongues will get deeper and deeper. And remember, you can speak in many different tongues.

(7) Try shouting in tongues for thirty minutes each day for three days, and see what God will do for you. From doing this, a sister in Christ moved into a whole new place of intercession, a brother from Ireland reported that his prayer life was transformed, and a television executive stated, "I am not the same person." You, too, will be changed.

A Door of Opportunity

Through the baptism in the Holy Spirit, a door of opportunity has been opened for you to walk in a deeper intimacy with God, to have a greater anointing in your life, and to begin to operate in the gifts of the Holy Spirit. Daily praising, worshipping and interceding in tongues is a supremely important key to walking through that door of opportunity. Expect to see your prayers answered, and more quickly. Remember, pray or sing at least thirty minutes daily in tongues. What a super blessing this will be to your life!

FREE FROM THE PAST

WHY SPEAK IN OTHER TONGUES SINCE IT IS A LANGUAGE YOU DON'T UNDERSTAND?

Many people ask this question, and there are many answers. Here are a few of them:

1. When we speak in tongues, we are speaking directly to God, in a real language, unknown to us, but inspired and directed by the Holy Spirit. *"For he that speaketh in an unknown tongue speaketh not unto men, but unto God: for no man understandeth him, howbeit in the spirit he speaketh mysteries"* (1 Corinthians 14:2).

2. Speaking in tongues is a language of God's glory, and so it opens the door into His presence.

3. Speaking in tongues also opens the door to inner transformation through inner healing and deliverance.

4. Because it brings an increase in the anointing, praying in the Spirit (speaking in tongues) increases our ability to understand, enjoy and believe the Word of God, and thereby our faith and wisdom are increased. When we speak in tongues, God puts into us wisdom, truth and understanding about spiritual and natural things—including marriage, child-raising, business affairs, even inventions and new ideas!

5. St. Paul considered speaking in tongues so important that he said, *"I thank my God, I speak with tongues more than ye all"* (1 Corinthians 14:18). Jesus said,

APPENDIX

"And these signs shall follow them that believe [That's you and me]; ... *they shall speak with new tongues;* ... *they shall lay hands on the sick, and they shall recover"* (Mark 16:17-18).

6. Speaking in tongues enables us to deeply praise and worship God, usually through singing in tongues.

7. Speaking in tongues empowers us to intercede for others and for ourselves more effectively because the Holy Spirit in us prays the perfect prayer in an unknown tongue through us (see Romans 8:26-27)! It is also the key to deep travail and self-travail.

8. Speaking in tongues also increases the power and presence of God within us, enabling us to pray and speak (or sing) more effectively in English. When the disciples were baptized in the Holy Spirit on the Day of Pentecost, *"They ... ALL began to speak with other tongues, as the Spirit gave them utterance"* (Acts 2:4, Emphasis added).

9. Speaking in tongues is the key to enabling us to function more effectively in one or more of the nine gifts of the Holy Spirit, including laying hands on the sick (see 1 Corinthians 12:8-10) and seeing God do miracles for them.

10. You can intercede in tongues for others. You can praise or worship God in tongues. You can receive answers

to questions by praying in tongues. You can do spiritual warfare in tongues.

11. Through praying intensely in tongues, a door will be opened, enabling you to ascend into the Third Heaven—before the throne of God. From this place, your intercession or worship will produce far greater results.

BEGIN TODAY

Begin today. Pray or sing in tongues seven minutes each day, and then quickly increase this time to thirty minutes or more as a new lifestyle. As you do this, expect wisdom, joy and peace to greatly increase in your life.

My wife, Pattie, and I pray in other tongues every day, and it has transformed our lives in many beneficial ways. This is a holy, awesome gift from God to us, and it's for you too. Reach out now and receive it, and allow it to become part of your daily life with God. It will dramatically affect your spiritual life and that of your children. Through the working of God's Spirit in you, you can be *Free from the Past*.

Ministry Page

If you desire us to minister in your church or home group, want to purchase our materials or give to our ministry, you may contact us in any of the following ways:

John Chappell
The Chappell Ministries, Inc.
P.O. Box 172
Bartow, FL 33831

E-mail: JChap777@aol.com

On the Web: www.laughcry.org

Telephone: (863) 221-1479
Cell: (863) 221-1479

— Notes —

Notes

CPSIA information can be obtained at www.ICGtesting.com
Printed in the USA
LVOW100706091012

302081LV00002B/4/P